The Living Page
Keeping Notebooks with Charlotte Mason

Laurie Bestvater

For Sarah, Samuel and Caleb,
my best teachers.
And for Bryan who is always just the right sort of man.

Contents

Acknowledgments

*"It is a tremendous act of violence to begin anything. I am not able to begin.
I simply skip what should be the beginning."*

– Rainer Maria Rilke

And so am I unable to begin, for in tracing the impact of Charlotte Mason's thought, who could say where the thread began? "Idea begets idea" and thus we are educated. Looking back I know where I have glimpsed the Glory along the way that has inspired me to examine the tapestry more fully. The work and love of my own family who intuitively offered so many of the good things Mason prescribes was perhaps the loom.

At Queen's University, Dr. William C. James was instrumental in helping me to see the importance of story, friendship, and the natural world to formation. Over thirty years ago he introduced me to Annie Dillard, Alice Walker, Margret Laurence and many other treasured voices I would have missed. I am still living in that luminous moment when Shug in *The Color Purple* says, "I think it pisses God off when you walk by the color purple in a field and don't notice it." That slightly shocking passage was underlined and copied and discussed but neither of us suspected how long it would take to become a Noticer or for those particular threads to look like anything.

Dr. Maureen Muldoon at the University of Windsor, Ontario, continually held before me a gracious and disciplined practice of ethics, a deep respect for the personhood and voice of the learner, even (especially?) in academia, and an unrelenting calm that was very appealing. I remember long discussions about the role of women in the Church and the place she was finding with the Quakers that seem, now, just the right warp and woof for the work I find myself compelled to do.

Later the Francis Schaeffer family and Susan's book, *For the Children's Sake*, invited me (and so many of us) to be about the work of ensuring children have stories, relish outdoor adventures, and are listened to carefully. And like so many of us, I read that iconic introduction to Mason with a small group of faithful friends and co-teachers. I was nourished by the excitement of sharing each "aha" as we went on to read Mason for ourselves and lived the discoveries with our own students in those early days. Jen, Jill, Ruth and Debbie were the initial recipients of my stumbling narrations long after my dear husband's eyes had glazed over.

I see woven in, the marvel of the emerging Internet that connected similar groups of kindred spirits across the world in the early nineties—particularly the selfless advisory of Ambleside Online, on whose shoulders so very many in the Mason community stand. And I see, in the last few years, the privilege of daily correspondence with a brilliant team of educators that set out to study deeply what Mason wrote in order to apply it in a culture begging for educational renewal. Sandy Rusby Bell, Jennifer Larnder Gagnon, Tammy Glaser, Rebekah Brown Hierholzer, Nicolle Hutchinson, Leslie Noelani Laurio, Dr. J. Carroll Smith, Dr. Jennifer Spencer, and Melanie Walker-Malone inspired and refined my thinking at every turn.

And of course, in the nature of things, I see my grown children, who are now the very fiber of these ideas in the next generation. You are each world changers and very dear. I am so grateful to you for my "bringing up."

I am no expert; as my children will tell you, I have gone haltingly down this road in fits and starts. I see myself as a captivated layperson gathering this material for exploration by the Mason community and others interested in formation. Neither am I the first to attempt a list of the notebooks Mason used. I have seen several posts on e-mail lists and forums over the years and have had many constructive, but sadly, undocumented conversations. I know Wendi Capehart was an early voice on notebooks. Deborah Miller has also done careful work in this area (and shared her remarkable penchant for dates), but there are unrecognized others who contributed to my understanding. As Pascal said, it "would be better to say 'our book,' 'our commentary,' 'our history'…because there is in (this work) … more of other people's than (my) own." — I am grateful to and in debt to all of them. I am also very thankful to those, led by Dr. Deani Van Pelt, who worked so hard to allow us greater access to Mason by establishing the Charlotte Mason Digital Collection through Redeemer University College in Ancaster, Ontario. Archivist Marlene Powers has been consistently gracious and helpful as I have rummaged through the images. Your work continues to inspire more reading and thinking.

I owe especial thanks to: Sarah Bestvater, Dr. Deani Van Pelt, and Victoria Waters for carefully reviewing parts of this manuscript and making much appreciated practical suggestions.

Publication would not have been possible without the expert editorial ministrations of Michelle Lovi of Odyssey Books, and fellow Mason explorer, Megan Hoyt. Thank you for understanding so well that a writer also needs a handhold.

Part Two of *The Living Page* owes much of its shape and content to long conversations with Melanie Walker-Malone, founder and head of Red Mountain Community School in Birmingham, Alabama. As I wrote the first half of the book the material was quickened through our friendship and Red Mountain's practice. The meditations on Time, Place, Relationship and Glory were part of a treasured dialectic that led to the establishment of prov.en.der, a series of formation weekends based on Mason's pedagogy. Through our individual reading of Mason, though we lived in different countries and were unknown to each other, these postures had become fundamental to both of us over the years, and yet it was our relationship that ultimately brought them to the fore and gave them names. I am so very thankful for the openness and hospitality of this community and Melanie's "fine art of standing aside," while I narrated the connections I was seeing with the notebooks. I have the courage to offer these words, not because they have any inherent goodness (and I take full responsibility for the errors and omissions!) but because somehow, one narration leads to another and you all have shown me again how curious things happen in that relationship as we all "get on" in our education.

Laurie Bestvater,
Deus est qui Deum Dat,
Pentecost, 2013

*"Perhaps this is one of the secrets of life—
to know 'glory' when we see it."*

– Charlotte M. Mason

*"What I had done, opening the journal, was to open a door,
or more truthfully, to become a door."*

– Hannah Hinchman

Preface

They were not going to school to learn where they were, let alone the pleasures and pains of being there, or what ought to be said there. You couldn't learn those things in a school. They went to school, apparently, to learn to say over and over again, regardless of where they were, what had already been said too often. They learned to have a very high opinion of God and a very low opinion of His works--although they could tell you this world had been made by God Himself. What they didn't see was that it is beautiful and some of the greatest beauties are the briefest.

– Wendell Berry[1]

This was my copy work today. The exercise was not about my penmanship and spelling as copy work is for beginners in British educationalist Charlotte Mason's design for education but, like her older students did, I keep a "Commonplace," a notebook that is my constant reading companion wherein I copy poems I like or passages from my latest reading or sometimes brief character sketches and lists.[2] It is a history, a personal record of my thinking. Because certain things strike me as meaningful and important depending on my current thinking or circumstances, my Commonplace (unwittingly started by a high school girl with an affinity for words and paper) will be nothing like yours; might even seem random and unimportant compared to your experience. For me, it has the power to recall my life journey in detail; each copied morsel is capable of evoking the whole feast I enjoyed at the time.

Let me see if I can trace the rabbit trail of connections I made when I knew I had to have this passage from Wendell Berry's *Jayber Crow* in my notebook. (Leave aside for now the fact that my son gave me the book for my birthday, so I was already predisposed to love it for all the years of Grand Conversation[3] we have enjoyed together and the fact that I am already very fond of Wendell Berry's poetry.) I was thinking about Mason's invitation to take this journey with my children as "students of Divinity." All the sweetness (and challenges, never doubt it!) of the years were before me as I read Jayber's thoughts about the seminary students coming to his town and how really ineffective he felt they were. I was thinking that real learning cannot happen because someone (in a seminary or not) prescribes it and pours it into us. I was thinking how "knowing where they were, and the pleasures and pains of being there" could refer to the inner landscape; Mason asserted that persons can only be built up from within. In Berry's words: "saying over and over again what had already been said too often," I recognized the sad way we expect children to grow by giving disembodied information and requiring parrot answers (especially in the Church) instead of arranging a diet rich in living ideas that might be less within our control but which might reflect the work of the Holy Spirit who is like the wind that comes and goes at will. The journey is a little risky, is it not? We want companions who recognize the landscape; that's why Jayber is so disappointed in the seminarians who could not see that "the world was beautiful." Isn't that why some of us resonate so deeply with Mason? She *can* see the beauty?

Then my mind flew again to the whole person Mason insists that the scriptures present, who would never live comfortably in a world that "has a very high opinion of God and a very low opinion of his works." Such a view, which many attribute to the thinking of the Enlightenment, degenerates into a dualism propagated by the Greeks that eventually came to divide the child into several faculties, and proceeded to try to fill his mind with "important" facts like it was a bucket while stealing away all the beauty and nourishment of a full, joyful human life.

I paused in my copying on the notion of seeing. "What they didn't see...." When did it happen? How is it that we do not see? What robs wonder? Did they go to school and learn not to see? Little children seem to see everything. If I hold a baby in my arms, invariably it will try to pick off the mole on my right cheek. A toddler simply *must* stop to watch the ants on his walk. What is it we do to close their eyes? And then I was right back where I started—notebooks.

> One thing at any rate we know with certainty, that no
> teaching, no information becomes knowledge to any of us
> until the individual mind has acted upon it, translated it,

transformed, absorbed it, to reappear, like our bodily food, in forms of vitality. Therefore, teaching, talk and tale, however lucid or fascinating, effect nothing until self-activity be set up; that is, self-education is the only possible education; the rest is mere veneer laid on the surface of a child's nature.[4]

Mason had shown me that the notebooks can be forms of vitality, literally the shape and outline, the liturgy of the attentive life. They nurture the science of relations and the art of mindfulness. They teach us to see the very brief beauty of now, to know the landscape of here, to be present in all our pleasures and pains. Through them we, haltingly, dwell in a world of ideas and connections with an ever-higher opinion of God and his works and as truer students of Divinity.

"Keepers of private notebooks are a different breed altogether, lonely and resistant rearrangers of things, anxious malcontents, children afflicted apparently at birth with some presentiment of loss," says Joan Didion in her iconic essay, "Keeping a Notebook."[5] Her self-deprecatory tone belies her real intent and this question that has occupied me for some time: Why do I have so many notebooks? Why do those who keep them, keep notebooks—and often more than one?[6] And how do notebooks serve Charlotte Mason's conception of education?

Mason refers specifically to several kinds of student-produced notebooks as integral to her approach in her six volumes on pedagogy, and others appear to have occurred to her as rather interesting possibilities. Overall, it is clear that she esteems this practice of "keeping a notebook." Imagine the conversation Mason might have with Didion. Mason might concede that students who keep notebooks are "a different breed" since she noticed "people are naturally divided into those who read and think and those who do not read and think."[7] (She might not commit to whether notebooks cause the thinking or the thinking causes the notebooks; certainly there are great thinkers who do not keep notebooks.) She might even agree that they are lonely; the readers and thinkers she nurtures might search a while to find true community, being bred on ideas as they are. As for being "resistant rearrangers," Mason would see that as a good thing: we read and, in our own personal way, we rearrange through narration for true knowing, and the results of that generative process may be seen in our notebooks.[8] If Mason's students are "anxious," it is for a full life; if "malcontents," it is in resisting the educational status quo. She called for an educational revolution.[9] If, as children, they were "afflicted with some presentiment of loss," she would say it is viral in all of us until we are educated out of it and that the loss is the ability to "know 'glory' when we see it."[10]

We cannot know for certain what Mason and Didion would say to each other, and in a few cases Mason's references to a particular notebook are incidental and must, for now, remain a mystery, but by looking at the nuances of her philosophy and carefully searching her work, it is possible to paint a rather remarkable picture of what she wanted from the various notebooks and student work she established. The following exploration in broad strokes depicts my personal grappling with her suggested forms of vitality that I hope may prove fruitful:

Chapter 1 The Art of the Keeper
Offers a brief consideration of notebook keeping in general.

Chapter 2 Gallery of Forms
Catalogues the many references to notebooks and other student work within Mason's writing and in the P.N.E.U. literature.

Chapter 3 The Grand Invitation
Draws some conclusions about the worth of the notebooks.

Chapter 4 "Setting up Self-Activity"
Examines the postures and implications of Keeping for our educational practice.

Chapter 5 R.S.V.P.—The Shape of Life
Contains meditations on living fully with the "forms of vitality."

Part One

1

The Art of the Keeper

" 'To Keep,' had become for Tracy the most important verb
in the English language.

'And it isn't only possessive,' she had defended herself against Bella.
'It means to watch over, take care of, maintain.' "

– Rumer Godden

"Art is life playing to other rhythms."

– Muriel Barbery

I have on my desk a small, thin, rather rustic notebook of handmade paper, its pages crudely bound with twine. I purchased it from a street vendor in Indonesia. My notebook denotes not only an interesting cultural trend but provides a clue to the history of notebook keeping. Leaving aside the poverty of that country and the attending predisposition for people of such cultures to create "artifacts" for wealthy western tourists, let us say the appeal of this particular notebook is its simplicity. In this fast and technologically spectacular culture, its charm lies in the fact that it is handmade and consequently I have saved it for some special personal lists. It has me thinking even more deeply about Didion's question, "Why do we keep notebooks?" This "primitive" notebook seems to suggest that some things have not changed: from time's beginning almost, to the current and still very popular notebook trends revealed by companies like Moleskine, people have wanted something to write on and a way to keep those writings together.[11]

Percy Leslie Waterhouse, writer of the classic well known to students of Architecture, *The Story of the Art of Building,* remarks that the tale of building begins with human life, "Man's earliest instinct would prompt him to provide himself with food and shelter."[12] The art of the notebook comes a little later, but not much; storytellers by nature, it would not be long, historically speaking, before someone somewhere felt the need to make a note— either to remember something for themselves or to tell it to someone else.

One of the earliest forms of bookbinding is thought to have originated in India around the fifth century BCE, perhaps earlier, where inventive people used something sharp (a stylus) to inscribe messages on dried leaves, later inking them over with the juice of plants in a relief-type printing process and tying the leaves together between boards bound with twine for preservation. However this great idea spread, possibly through Buddhist monks to Persia, Afghanistan, Iran, and China, it is certain the Egyptians had papyrus and scrolls, the Mayan's kept "books," and the Hebrews, Greeks, and Romans had scrolls and papers for their important thoughts.[13] Long before blogs citing savvy farmers keeping pocket notebooks to list their "rainy day work," indeed, before humankind was even agricultural, we were responding, apparently, to a need to "keep a notebook."[14]

Waterhouse also notes that the buildings, the "literature in stone and marble," that lived to tell the story of a culture are typically, almost exclusively, "outcomes of the nation's religious beliefs."[15] It is just so with the notebook: dwellings, being built to last only the length of a man's life or his family's, were not enduring structures and neither did his daily thoughts and plans, if recorded at all, survive the wear of time. As with Architecture, we cannot reconstruct bookbinding's earliest days with clarity but it is clear that the religious thought of a culture, besides spurring the greatest buildings, is also the impetus of actual book making. Not surprisingly, all those early troubles to make paper and print were kept for the culture's most important discoveries and thoughts, the existential questions if you will, not the shopping lists.[16] Egyptian priestly texts populated their costly papyrus scrolls; the Mayan Codex was what that people troubled itself to write; Romans and Greeks inscribed their funeral rites and laws, and eventually the Hebrews and Christians took things to a high literary pitch in the West, enjoined by scripture to "record the vision, And inscribe *it* on tablets." (Hab 2:2 New American Standard)

If we speed over the faithfulness of the monastic scribes and give a quick nod to the invention of the printing press and the Gutenberg Bible, the rest is history: composition books and blank journals are now readily available at every big box and corner store, available so inexpensively as to be common and ironic as we reach that digital dominion, the projected "paperless culture."[17] Shall we despair of the future of the notebook? Is Didion's question of 1966, indeed Mason's practice, an anachronism? Why now, in an age where one's thoughts and pictures, doings and strivings are so easily recorded with a smart phone or blog, and students in even the youngest classrooms are handed electronic tablets with textbooks loaded and worksheets at the ready, bother to look into the art of keeping notebooks? Is perhaps the attraction to Mason's methods and my persistent love for notebooks just a luddite tendency that needs to be addressed, or is there something indispensable in the keeping of notebooks, an art without which human beings would be the poorer?

Even in a cursory look at history, especially at the unfolding of technology, the original need for paper and pencil seems obvious. But with current leanings towards technology in the classroom, how can we be certain that notebooks are not now just a sentimental harkening to the past? Mason has been a faithful guide in my educational journey so far, but Didion gives pause. *Is* there a point in keeping Mason's classroom practices in paper for this generation? As usual, as we follow Mason, we land in the philosophical realm with The Great Conversation. In innocently pondering, "why keep notebooks?" we awaken several of the Perennial Questions: "What is the nature of man?" "What is education?" "What does human flourishing look like?" "How far can technology properly take us in that direction?"

Fortunately, we are not left to flounder in a metaphysical abyss. Mason spends a great deal of time in her volumes describing her foundations, grounding her philosophy and practice convincingly on natural law. After fifty years of observing children and testing her ideas, she maintains there are laws that govern education just as physical laws govern the universe. To ignore them is like trying to make cream puffs without a recipe by just assembling the flour and the butter and the salt on the counter. "We labour under the mistake of supposing that there is no *natural law* or inherent principle according to which a child's course of studies should be regulated; the education we offer is too utilitarian."[18] She makes claims about human nature: "We are *so made* that only those ideas and arguments which we go over are we able to retain."[19] (emphasis mine) And she defines education and establishes a methodology in keeping with a vision for human flourishing:

> In the nature of things the unspoken demand of children is for a wide and very varied curriculum; it is necessary that they should have some knowledge of the wide range of interests proper to them as human beings and for no reasons of convenience or time limitations may we curtail their proper curriculum.[20]

Mason's dependence on some few ontological statements can seem deceptively simple: "The child is a person." "Education is an atmosphere, a discipline and a life." "Education is the Science of Relations." But each affirmation has layers of meaning and almost endless depths to sound for application to our practice.[21] Always she is bringing us back to an assertion of this natural law which she tested as diligently as any scientist of her age. Just before her death in 1923 Mason asserts in *A Philosophy of Education*, published posthumously, "I should like to add that no statement that I have advanced in the following volume rests upon opinion only. Every point has been proved in thousands of instances, and the method may be seen to work in many schools, large and small, Elementary and Secondary."[22]

As truth claims usually are, this *is* a rather audacious statement: "people are slow to understand that there is *no part* of a child's work at school which some philosophic principle does not underlie."[23] (emphasis mine) I have rested here for a very long time. Since nothing in Mason's writings gives any sense of a tendency to exaggeration and, on the contrary, she insists on the habit of "strict veracity" for her students, I must assume she is resolute.[24] "No part of our practice" means not only that she has tested these paper postures and found them essential, but also that what she calls the forms of vitality are themselves grounded in demonstrable philosophical principles which by definition would have to be counted as timeless. If Mason is asking those big questions about some seemingly innocuous student work, there seems no way around it; she is proposing the art of keeping a notebook as Something True.

We do not have to take her word for it, however. The nice thing about a natural law is that it is, by definition, testable. It should turn out to be true in all settings. Though this treatment cannot include the studies required for a definitive educational or psychological statement on the matter, even the briefest historical survey will give us an inkling of the field to be tried: it certainly appears the correlation of notebook keepings to people of amazing achievement is more than anecdotal.

Surely in the realm of science, the practice of keeping notebooks has proven remarkable. Linus Pauling, as Wikipedia reports, was a renowned 20th century "chemist, biochemist, peace activist, author, educator" and two-time Nobel Prize winner. He left forty-seven research journals at his death in 1994.[25] His notebooks span fifty years and include everything from the expected laboratory proceedings to personal anecdotes, correspondence, travel notes, and ideas for future projects.

Going farther back, the University of Melbourne is reporting that Galileo and his notebooks, kept over four hundred years ago, are even more of a treasure than originally thought. Apparently, no one recognized until recently that his notebooks testify that Galileo identified Neptune two hundred thirty-four years before it was officially "discovered."[26]

Thomas Edison was also a Keeper. He and his lab associates created more than three thousand notebooks! Interestingly, "not all of Edison's notebooks are experimental in nature. Some of the earliest books contain accounting records, and sometimes experimental and financial material are indiscriminately mixed together in the same book, many of them containing beautiful drawings."[27]

Likewise, Alexander Graham Bell, Albert Einstein, and Nikola Tesla (inventor of the "death beam," the concept weapon made of particles), were notorious Keepers. They all left the science community volumes of incredible worth, except for Tesla who is believed to have kept notebooks that have been mysteriously missing since the day of his death. Apparently, those were worthy enough to be stolen!

Keepers of nature notebooks and field journals also have a long history, especially women who often had little other access to the realms of science. These books were often cherished for field notes, geographical sketches and realistic botanical paintings. Maria Sibylla Merian (1647-1717), sometimes called the first female scientist and the mother of entomology, before Henri Fabre even, is one of the earliest of such Western examples.[28] Merian was an acute observer who as a young girl tested and challenged the Greek notion that insects are born out of the mud by capturing and documenting the lifecycle of the many butterflies and caterpillars around her home in Germany against virulent charges of witchcraft. She did not separate science and art (as Mason's Nature Notebook does not) but created many wonderful flower and insect designs based on her drawings for her family's textile business.[29]

Closer to Mason's time, if not country, is Thoreau, with fourteen known volumes of field studies made around his beloved Walden Pond. Beatrix

Potter, a neighbor of Mason's House of Education and champion of the beauty of the local Lake District farm lands, was an illustrator par excellence of the sweet anthropomorphic animals, Peter Rabbit and his friends. She was noticing and drawing the local flora and fauna from an early age. Edith Holden, also of Mason's time, created paintings much like those made by House of Education students.[30] It was a "thing" in those days, to be sure. Ladies painted.[31]

But the practice continued to be attractive to naturalists. Rachel Carson was a Keeper, as were Georgia O'Keefe and William Beebe of Bronx Zoo fame. Materials might have differed a little, but subject matter and impulse did not. Ansel Adams, the celebrated American nature photographer, once remarked, "No photographer should be without one!"[32] And the notebooks of such devoted and careful naturalists continue to inspire; John Muir alone has seventy-eight journals which are still being enjoyed daily through the Internet and digital technology.

Certainly in the ages of great exploration, the writings and drawings of men like Columbus, Magellan and Livingston link keen observation and careful recording. Meriwether Lewis created notebooks described as "a record of national Treasure."[33] Where would we be without the accounts of Perry, Amundsen and Darwin's celebrated records of his time in the Galapagos? Their scrutiny and notation of the history, flora and fauna, geography and cultures they encountered in their journeys are inestimably rich possessions in those respective fields. Mason herself follows suit with her five volume series known as *The Ambleside Geographies*, along with her 1881 publication *The Forty Shires: Their History, Scenery, Arts and Legends*—several of these cherish the areas of England she walked and knew so intimately.

Neither does the urge for the blank page occur to just the scientific mind. Indeed, it seems curiosity is the first symptom of what Didion calls, "this affliction." Da Vinci, of course, blurred the distinction between science and art mixing gorgeous, intimate drawings of the human form with his fantastical inventions in his notebooks. Stories about his need to see the glory of the human body having led to his stealing of cadavers are well known; certainly he was doing some very detailed "rearranging" and noticing!

Thomas Jefferson was a great noticer who, among other things, loved measurements. His various interests made him an early adopter of a Victorian sort of pocket notebook, an innovation sometimes known as an "Aide Memoire." Typically, such a "notebook" would contain six tiny reusable, ivory "pages"—one for each working day of the week. (One did not take notes on Sundays!) Ladies sometimes had such a "notebook" and pencil on a chain, or on a collection of chains and useful artifacts, known as a "Chatelaine," which was invented to deal with their paucity of pockets and often pinned at the waist as were housekeeping keys.[34] "Back in his Cabinet, or office, he (Jefferson) later copied the information into any of seven books in which he kept records about his garden, farms, finances, and other concerns; he then erased the writing in the ivory notebook.[35]

Jefferson kept legal and literary commonplaces, nature and garden notebooks almost a century before Mason. Many of his contemporaries did. Harvard University allows for the use of commonplaces by intellectuals as far back as medieval times.[36] Others, like professor of Rhetoric and Modern Composition Theory, Dr. Lynee Gaillet, trace it to the Greek and Roman exploration of rhetoric.[37] Suffice it to say the Commonplace has been known as a personal notebook and means for many centuries and in many countries of indexing the common places wherein wisdom could be located.

> They became significant in Early Modern Europe. "Commonplace" is a translation of a Latin term *locus communis* which means a "theme or argument of general application," such as a statement of proverbial wisdom. In this original sense commonplace books were collections of such sayings, such as John Milton's commonplace book. Scholars have expanded this usage to include any manuscript that collects material along a common theme by an individual. Such books were essentially scrapbooks filled with items of every kind: medical receipts, quotes, letters, poems, tables or weights and measures, proverbs, prayers, legal formulae. Commonplaces were used by readers, writers, students, and humanists as an aid for remembering useful concepts or facts they had learned, and each commonplace was unique to its creator's particular interests.[38]

Harvard houses a special collection of commonplaces, including those of undergraduates from the 19th century, testifying to how the practice became an expectation of the intellectual life in America at the time that Mason was writing. Gaillet lists many well-known writers who have kept commonplaces; E.M. Forster, W.H. Auden, Oscar Wilde, Thomas Hardy, Wallace Stevens, George Gissing are a few of the classics.[39]

But commonplaces are not only of the past. Recently, distinguished Canadian singer/songwriter, Bruce Cockburn, donated the artifacts associated with his long career to McMaster University in Hamilton, Ontario. Among the guitars, posters, and band T-shirts are 32 eclectic notebooks kept from 1969-2002 "in which Cockburn wrote many of his songs, as well as snippets of poetry and day-to-day observations…(that) offer insight into how Cockburn worked his songwriting craft. 'That process is documented in the mongrel assortment of stationery that is now in the hands of McMaster,' he said."[40]

So, as Mason says of herself overall, she was not an innovator in this regard either.[41] The Keepers who were scholars, the movers and the shakers in science, the arts, and exploration on whom she called regularly in her classroom, she knew enough to imitate. To that extent, Mason comes to the art of keeping notebooks naturally, not in a vacuum but within the rich context of the Western notion of Liberal Arts which fairly demands some of these academic disciplines.

Other educators were very likely recognizing similar things. It remains to be seen to what extent such notebooks were part and parcel of a Victorian child's classroom experience. (If indeed that child had any schooling at all; many poor children did not.) An in-depth positioning of Mason's pedagogy within the educational thought of the day would likely reveal many interesting side roads and discoveries. In so many ways, Mason was, and could not help but be, a product of her time, often echoing or refining ideas found in Comenius, Pestalozzi, Froebel, Herbart, Ruskin, Matthew Arnold, the men known as "the Scottish school of philosophers" as well as various other intellectuals and sages. She addresses her concerns and points of disagreement with many of them in her volumes and in *The Parents' Review*, and the community gathering around Mason's work today is beginning to piece together the ways in which she was shaped by and contributed to her intellectual climate.

In the use of notebooks, however, it is not hard to imagine Mason beginning by collecting "best practices" just like the rest of us. We know she credits G. Bernau with the Book of Centuries and Francis Buss was using history charts.[42] Copybooks were common in the turn of the century classroom but, as is often revealed to be the case with Mason, her take on them was not. Though not my primary concern here, further work will likely reveal the origins of each of her initial notebook acquisitions. In this brief treatment I hope, in light of her claims of every practice having its principle, to get at the root of *why* she admired these paper postures and how she saw them working within her philosophical framework and not so much the movements and ideas that fed that understanding. The reader will forgive me if I admit that there is an a profound worth to comprehending the societal and historical context in which Mason's ideas took hold at the same time as I leave such a picture in the hands of those more capable than I to paint it.

Similarly, I am not able to delve overmuch into our current educational climate and how Mason's ideas may or may not coincide with modern thinkers and movements except to notice that educational thought does tend to swing widely, and the current position of the pendulum in the West may explain the appeal of Mason's re-emergence.[43] Her method has arrived like a time capsule filled with ideas we seem to be in danger of losing track of in this fill-in-the-blank, megabyte world. "Blog journals are the fastest growing form of journal keeping," says researcher Jennifer New.[44] Spiritual formation consultant Sharon Ely Pearson writes, "We are no longer shackled to books and paper. Books may become outdated."[45] Shackled? Innovator or no, perhaps we simply have need of a studied, intelligent, commonsense voice from the past asking us to hold up for a minute and examine the force of the culture shapers she insisted on as a curriculum for every child and the particular paper ways they had of pursuing their loves.

Neither do I wish to suggest that Mason did not have feet of clay like the rest of us; this is precisely why her work has such worth. She lived it with all the foibles and challenges of a human life; hers was not just a pristine theory sprung fully formed from the head of Zeus. More thorough scholarship around her life can only bring that into sharper focus. There has been a tendency to see only the crinoline and lace, tea and poetry of Mason's days and so to miss some of the import of her scholarship and the seriousness of her proposals. The assumption can sometimes be that Mason's appeal is only to romantics and late adopters. Mason historian, Margaret Coombs, can only joke wryly about e-mail because this is the case.

> (Charlotte Mason) readily absorbed new ideas throughout her life up to and after her move to Ambleside in 1891, which influenced her thinking and, as you know, read or was read to all the time. She even mentions Marx in "An

Essay," but I do not see her as a modernist—she loved the Victorian values, and I think she would have got Elsie Kitching to send her emails!! [46]

But two questions continue to niggle if we put forward only Victorian values and take Mason as simply representative of her time, or someone from whom we may perhaps gather some effective techniques for the classroom. Though Mason does admire "a golden deed," a marvelous discovery, the mind of a great artist, and hopes her children will do the same, is that *all* she is after in the classroom—"secrets to success," as it were? Being so vociferous against a utilitarian education and anything smacking of a system would Mason be apt to write today, *Classroom Paper Practices: The Da Vinci Technique?* Over and over again, ideas like being "educated by our desires," how much the student "cares," "a full human life," and "seeing glory" appear in her writings. What shall we do about these?

Though we have barely skimmed the surface, there is little doubt in even a perfunctory look that some of the most amazing of the world's treasured artifacts and ideas have come from notebook Keepers. Yet, from Bach and Beethoven to Bob Dylan, from Gerard Manley Hopkins to Annie Dillard and Billy Collins, is it not the Keeper's full human life that Mason esteems? What if the emphasis is meant to be on the formative process—the growing person who feasts upon and then shares the Great Ideas in creating the art, rather than the artifact or achievement itself?

And second, if Mason's proposal of a natural law of education is putative, then must not every practice have its grounding principle and the forms of vitality be acknowledged as an essential way of working with (and not against) what Mason recognized as "a law of mind?"[47] This second question touches on what could be considered Mason's unique contribution to the literature of Keepers—her ever-present regard of children. Although many of the current works on Keeping acknowledge similar reasons for and outcomes of the notebook habit, there is very little written about children as Keepers. And, while anecdotal evidence at least shows that many thinking people have been "successful" and productive keeping notebooks, it remains to be seen how such disciplines were used in other schools in Mason's time. Undoubtedly, young girls of a certain class would have learned to paint and scholars reading at the universities made use of commonplaces, but were there any other educators relying on these forms of vitality as heavily for children? If not, why not? And then why did she?

If Mason is unique at all, it is in her simple but profound insistence that we regard the child a born person. If one is going to propose universal laws of education (natural laws) for human-kind and assert that children are made of the exact same stuff as grown people, children are not "oysters" or going-to-be-persons, etc., but simply less experienced persons who feel, analyze, generalize, and compare for themselves, then the requirement is (quite shockingly) to allow them access to the "literature of grown up people," what we've learned to call, the Great Books, and through those classics to the Great Conversation.[48] I am proposing that it is with the forms of vitality that Mason makes an appeal even more explicit and revolutionary. Deep within the Great Books, inside the Great Conversation, she sees what I am calling, "The Grand Invitation." With no qualms, no holds barred, Charlotte Mason through her Great Recognition and ensuing pledge to "masterly inactivity" allows the quiet persistence of the forms of vitality to invite children to notice and discuss the Perennial Questions, to be delvers into existential matters for themselves. The *teleos* or end of education, as she puts it, is to become "students of Divinity." Even children. It is more than preposterous.

The question, then, as interesting as that answer will be, is not so much did any other Victorian teacher use these kinds of notebooks? But who of us dares do it even now, years after Mason stands up (whether on the shoulders of others or not), as the first child-centered educator.[49]

A simple Google search reveals how very little is being published on children and notebook keeping. One can find various teachers' guides for journaling in the classroom or bookmaking. But even if they avoid the notion that such a journal is to be filled with "self," these are invariably about facilitating creative writing projects, *creating authors*—one-offs designed for a specific purpose and largely utilitarian. Authors like Catherine Stonehouse and Scottie May are too rare, might even pass as disciples of Mason, when they recognize in *Listening to Children on the Spiritual Journey*, the delicate dance of respectful support required in a true learning community.

> Our commitment to provide instruction and guidance must be balanced by respect for the child that flows from the deeply held belief that each child is fully human and made in the image of God. We will want to listen to discern where God is at work, what we can learn from the child, and how we can partner with God in the formation of each unique and precious girl or boy.[50]

In our day, this is so much easier said than done, and even fewer realize that the materials we give our children will have an implicit message and can serve to open the way to formation or close it firmly.[51] Jennifer New and Danny Greggory, with his successful website and book, *An Illustrated Life,* write very convincingly about adult Keepers. They have recognized the imperative: "Not surprisingly, several contributors talked about their journals as a meditative process. Kenny says, 'I work in my journal every day. If I don't, I feel a void. It's like a prayer or meditation.' "[52] Gregory quotes artist Rick Beerhorst who notices, "my journal helps me remain sensitive to my surroundings. Drawing in my sketchbook quiets me down, slows me down so I am more able to hear the quiet voice of God speaking through the ordinary things and situations. It's like tracing the thumb-prints He left all over the crowded world."[53]

Adams claimed no naturalist should be without. Theologian Richard Foster, poet Luci Shaw, Ron Klug, author of *How to Keep a Spiritual Journal,* and many others realize that "no student of Divinity" should be without one. Charlotte Mason, under her usual banner, takes what is set aside for the enlightened and scholarly and offers it to children, "the least of these," saying, in effect, "no child should be without one." If "education is of the spirit," Mason's forms of vitality are an essential means of grace that invite this mysterious unfolding and growth.[54]

~~~~~~~

I can picture another notebook on my desk. Sadly, it was lost in a move. It was far more precious than any I share at workshops or describe on my blog but so plain as to be in disguise—a glance at my desk, were it there, and you could easily miss it. I have kept a commonplace off and on since high school driven by nothing more than the power, beauty, and aptness of words to try and capture that rare glimpse of what I know now to call glory, but I can trace my becoming the "rearranger" Didion describes even farther back to a cheap, primary Hilroy "scribbler" with blue lines and a scruffy orange cover. It was one of my dearest belongings. Only a few of the yellowed and slightly grubby pages were written on, and the washed out magic marker that filled them belied my notebook's import.

As an only child until I was nearly twelve, an aunt, my senior by seven years, filled in for an older sister. Since we lived far apart, unlike sisters, our time together was never long enough to result in ennui or struggle, and

I would literally count the days until I could travel to my grandmother's house (itself a refuge and a joy) to bask in the love and company of this dear companion. Sensitive and kindhearted enough to bother with a younger child so willingly, my aunt shared her fingernail polish, took me to the village skating rink, bought me "chips with vinegar" at the chip truck, and walked me to Buster's corner store with my quarter hot in my hand to pick out a brown paper bag of penny candy. On this particular trip, I had been anticipated. Realizing how I cherished our days together, my dear aunt had thought of us keeping a journal of the visit. After dinner the first evening, she produced the exercise book, likely bought at Kresge's Dime Store, and wrote (me snuggled beside her in the cozy plaid reclining chair), "Day One" in her beautiful script across the top of the first set of pages.

Somehow she knew that filling all those lines with words might sink even an eager beginning journalist, so we started with a drawing of the pork chops we had just had for supper and we walked backwards through the day, stopping to draw a skate to represent the rink along with the word "skating," the Peppermint Patty in Grandpa's pocket for me when he arrived from work, and the coloring book and crayons we had shared that morning while the household was being put to rights. The Brothers Grimm that lay in the fat, red *Children's Story Hour* giving support under "our" journal was waiting for the coveted before bedtime read. I drew and she drew and sometimes we printed. They were very ordinary things that we recorded, but it was to me a magic I would be infected by all my life.

I trundled my treasure home. I kept it for years. It was a simple, mostly graphic memory, but though it had only a few pictures and even fewer words, through it I could recall all the feelings, sights, and smells of those ten days. But mostly what I carried away was the sense that I was import-ant. I had been taken seriously. In giving me a way to keep the ordinary days of the trip, I am sure no great academic progress was made; no great thoughts were captured; no wonderful manuscript produced, but I was encouraged to notice and somehow newly awake to the preciousness of time and the import of each daily incarnational encounter with Glory.

Reading Mason has helped me to know why notebook keeping would eventually grow into my own quiet discipline and the relationship and love in that one sacrificial but simple act of writing *with me* for several days invited me to become not only a writer but a "student of Divinity." A few years later, when my aunt gave me a poster for the back of my bedroom door so that I regularly fell asleep to Emily Dickinson's avowal, "or help one fainting robin into his nest again" no moral imperative needed to accompany it. I *knew* that Love notices. I *knew* already what the "poor robin" looked like. Mason is right: Education is of the spirit and reading and writing are somehow part of the magic.

Richard Foster says about reading and writing, "knowing truth is good, becoming truth is better."[55] He noticed by observing his own growth the need for that "ancient practice of *lectio divina*...to read with all my emotion, all my mind, all my heart, to read with every muscle, every nerve, every cell of my body."[56] It is through this kind of reading that "deep calls to deep," he said. Mason is banking on it. She is determined all her children will have what Aunt Betty unwittingly gave me; a blank page with the confidence that deep *will* call unto deep, even in the little child whom Jesus took upon His knee, saying, in effect: There is Glory out there; make it "visible and plain."

2

Gallery of Forms

"We all have need to be trained to see, and to have our eyes opened before we can take in the joy that is meant for us in this beautiful life."

– Charlotte Mason

"Art enables us to find ourselves and lose ourselves at the same time."

– Thomas Merton

What do we make then of these myriad ways to attend and make Glory "visible and plain?" In this chapter, we will create a catalogue, incomplete to be sure, of the various notebooks that appear in Mason's writings. While we cannot know exactly what was going on in the Parent's Union Schools and the nurseries of the P.N.E.U. membership or what the House of Education teachers were taught about student work, we do have some very interesting descriptions to examine. References in Mason's volumes along with samples in the archives and expanding access to *The Parents' Review* mean we can start to assemble a meaningful collection.[57] There is undoubtedly more to come, but it is not necessary to have a complete record for the snippets, taken together, to reveal some intriguing patterns and distinctions.

Nature Notebooks

Most who know Charlotte Mason through her North American re-emergence in the 1980s are familiar with her Nature Notebook. Mason's biographer, Essex Cholmondley, records Mason as its originator and a House of

Education student, Miss O'Farrell, confirms its early use across the curriculum and that Lord Baden-Powell, founder of the Boy Scout movement, credited Mason as his inspiration.[58]

> In connection with Natural History, every child in the P.U.S. keeps a Nature Book in which he paints from nature flowers, birds, insects, animals—in short, any natural object which takes his fancy—and he writes his own descriptions and notes, not those dictated by his teacher. Children who are too small to write dictate their notes, which are written down for them.
>
> Older children make lists of birds and flowers—and sometimes of mosses, fungi, sea-weeds, etc.—with their English and Latin names, Natural Orders, and date and place of finding. Probably few people know that this idea of Nature Notebooks which is now used in so many schools was not thought of until started by Miss Mason, and that it was from ideas of Miss Mason's that Sir Robert Baden-Powell kindly says he got many of his ideas upon scouting.[59]

Apparently, Mason already knows about children what Baden-Powell was just realizing at that time. He says:

> We then made the discovery that boys, when trusted and relied on, were just as capable and reliable as men. Also, from experience of the Boys' Brigade, I realised that men could be got voluntarily to sacrifice time and energy to training boys. Then my idea that Scouting could be educative was strengthened also, through the following incident. General Lord Allenby was riding to his house after a field day when his little son shouted to him, "Father, I have shot you; you are not half a Scout. A Scout looks upward as well as around him—you never saw me." There was the boy, sitting up in a tree overhead; but far above him, near the top of the tree, was his new governess. "What on earth are you doing up there?" cried the General. "Oh, I am teaching him Scouting," she said. She had been trained at Miss Charlotte Mason's College for Teachers, and they had

been using my book, *Aids to Scouting*, written for soldiers, as a textbook in the art of educating children.[60]

Thus it would seem that from the beginning, the Nature Notebook was not just about dry brush technique or a sweet Victorian pastime, rather it was a symbol of much of Mason's pedagogy: her respect for children, her early leanings toward "scouting," and her commitment to the outdoor classroom and nature as teacher.[61]

> As soon as he is able to keep it himself, a nature-diary is a source of delight to a child. Every day's walk gives him something to enter; three squirrels in a larch tree, a jay flying across such a field, a caterpillar climbing up a nettle, a snail eating a cabbage leaf, a spider dropping suddenly to the ground, where he found ground ivy, how it was growing and what plants were growing with it, how bindweed or ivy manages to climb. Innumerable matters to record occur to the intelligent child. While he is still quite young (five or six), he should begin to illustrate his notes freely with brush drawings; he should have a little help at first in mixing colours, in the way of principles, not directions. He should not be told to use now this and now that, but "we get purple by mixing so and so," and then he should be left to himself to get the right tint. As for drawing, instruction has no doubt its time and place; but his nature diary should be left to his own initiative.[62]

The number of phrases like, "source of delight," "keep it himself," "where he found," "occur to the intelligent child," "left to himself," "left to his own initiative," is arresting in so short a passage. Yes, painting is included, but the Nature Notebook is so much more than the sum of its parts—Mason's approach to children's need for play and meditation, her feeling that nature is their inheritance, her respect for them as people, her continual scaffolding of their seeing and "knowing glory" are evident even as early as 1896 and the writing of *Home Education*.[63] The Nature Notebooks represent a way of life—a lifetime habit formed "as soon as he is able" but essentially an approach to Nature and consequently, to Science, indeed, all of life, through that habit.

> The nature note-books which originated with the P.U.S. have recommended themselves pretty widely as travelling companions and life records wherein the 'finds' of every season, bird or flower, fungus or moss, is sketched, and described somewhat in the manner of Gilbert White. The nature notebook is very catholic and finds room for the stars in their courses and for, say, the fossil anemone found on the beach at Whitby. Certainly these notebooks do a good deal to bring science within the range of common thought and experience; we are anxious not to make science a utilitarian subject.[64]

This reference to Gilbert White is a strong clue as to what Mason wants. White (1720–1793), a curate known for his ornithology and nature journals, predates Mason. Today he is recognized as one of England's first ecologists, and tourists often visit his house and gardens in Shelborne. Something in his approach is the impetus for Mason's practice—perhaps his non-utilitarian interest and the variety of his entries.

Looking over reproductions of his journals one sees surprisingly few illustrations and a wide variety of annotations. For example, White's note for June 8, 1770 has above it a pretty sketch of a dragonfly on a reed, but that is the only illustration for June in that year. Perhaps it was his on-going relationship with a relatively small patch of country over time, allowing him to form deep knowledge of a particular place and to notice even the smallest seasonal changes that Mason admires. The complete annotation is reproduced below with my interpretive surmises in italics.

June 1770
Friday 8
291/2 3/10; 55 SE *(weather noted, wind etc.)* **S, SW. Sun, Shady.**
Sorbus aucuparia *(Latin for Rowan or Mountain Ash)*
S! foin begins to blow *(may refer to a field of ripening fodder)*
Scarabaeus auratus *(Latin name of a type of beetle)*
Melons begin to swell [65]

Though it is not clear that Mason desires a direct imitation of White, it seems his journaling helped spawn one of the earliest "inquiry based" models of school Science.[66] She says the Nature Notebook is about students learning "what to observe and mak(ing) discoveries for themselves, original so far as they are concerned."[67]

> The children keep a dated record of what they see in their nature note-books, which are left to their own management and are not corrected. These note-books are a source of pride and joy, and are freely illustrated by drawings (brush-work) of twig, flower, insect, etc. The knowledge necessary for these records is not given in the way of teaching.[68]

Cholmondley reproduces the whole passage from *Home and School Education* that describes all that the Nature Notebooks signify and using the terms Nature study and Science interchangeably.[69] Again the "catholicity"[70] of the things being included in these student-generated accounts is revealed: names of plants or stones or constellations leading to classification, tidbits about a plant's gesture, habitat, flowering and fruiting, recognition of a bird by flight and song and times of coming and going, and the time of year one may come upon certain "friends" in nature. The nature notebook is a dated observation of the progression of the seasons week to week, including drawings, prose, and information gathered on a need to know basis. It can include geology, geography, the course of the sun, behavior of clouds, weather signs and many other observations.

As the digitization of the Armitt Mason Archive and Museum brings greater access to the Charlotte Mason Collection, we can examine for ourselves what Mason describes in several intriguing examples wrought by her student teachers. As study continues, no doubt even finer nuances will be discerned. For instance, a long prose entry about a walk and then an evening lecture on insects, both given by a Rev. Mr. Thornley whom, we are told, often visited and assessed the nature notebooks of the senior student teachers gives a sense of the teachers' delight in their Nature work.[71] In one, there is an intriguing hand-sketched map of the constellations with unsigned poetry about the heavens included—perhaps the author's own? Another page is filled by a lovely dry brush painting of a tulip with the wry comment hinting at the effort required in building this notebook habit:

> I am horrified to find I have not written in my diary for nearly a month. After all, there are some things more important than nature notes but I am glad the meteorology

reports do not depend upon my daily observations. The weather is so bad that we have not dared to venture into the fields and have been reduced to painting garden flowers. Even the gaudy tulip. It was a relief however to get good big petals to work at—the field flowers now are so very tiny.[72]

Nature Notebook Lists

But a habit it very clearly was. The flower and bird lists the students kept in the back indicate just how frequently they must have walked and how carefully they observed.[73] Tabbed in the back of the Nature Notebook for the years which that book covered there would be headings: Birds, Flowers, etc., each having their own title page and student's records of scores of sightings with various details. In the photo below, (fig. 1) the student includes the common name of the flower, the Latin name and order, two years' worth of spaces by month for listing numbers of plants seen, along with a spot to record where they were growing.[74]

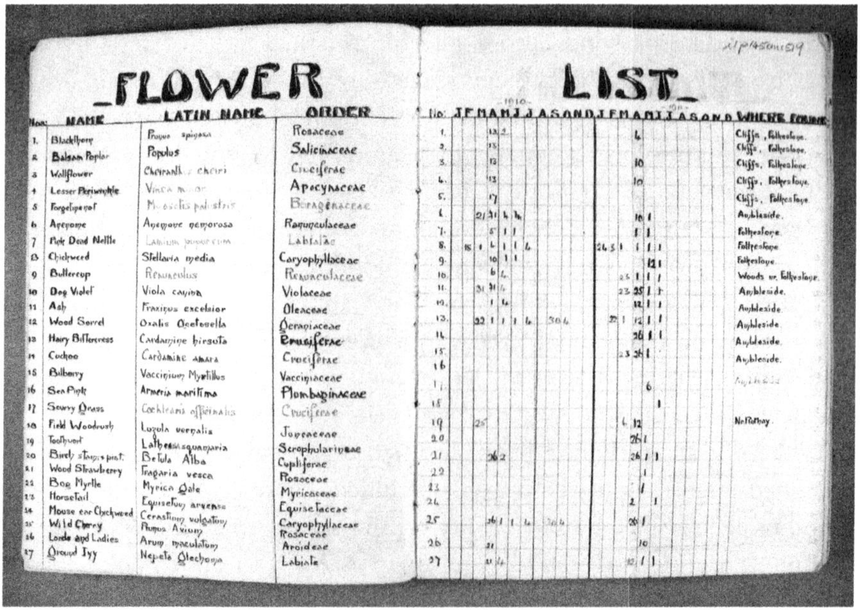

Fig. 1 Deck Flower Lists (*Image used under license from the Charlotte Mason Digital Collection, Redeemer University College, Ancaster, Ontario, Canada.*)

We cannot miss the importance of Mason's originality and emphasis here. If "we consider the skill of observation, perhaps the most fundamental scientific skill," as educational researcher, Brenda Rees, claims, Mason's Parents' Union Schools would by all counts have to be reckoned as serious about science.[75] Not only did students keep their own "life lists" there were also composite lists kept by the House of Education over many years creating a remarkably detailed record of local flora and fauna.[76]

The lists seem to vary slightly for plants and birds (and likely insects); perhaps they even varied among students, suggesting that there is more than one way to record what was wanted. Figure 2 below is a possible model for tracking birds. Rather than the date of the sighting, the boxes could just as easily be given to the number of sightings—the counting of populations. Or the emphasis might be on varieties and where they were observed, necessitating a somewhat different set up for the list. Mason does not appear rigid in this respect.

Common Name	Latin Name	Location	Jan	Feb	Mar	Apr	May	Jun
Cardinal	cardinalis	Service berry					25th	
Turkey Buzzard	Cathartes- aura	Newton Rd.						7th

Fig. 2. Sample Set Up for Bird Lists (design Laurie Bestvater)

Scrapbooks/Collections

Mason quotes none other than Herbert Spencer as inspiration for the classroom practice of scrapbooks and collecting.

> Think you that the rounded rock marked with parallel scratches calls up as much poetry in an ignorant mind as in the mind of the geologist, who knows that over this rock a glacier slid a million of years ago? The truth is, that those who have never entered on scientific pursuits are blind to most of the poetry by which they are surrounded. Whoever has not in youth collected plants and insects, knows not half the halo of interest which lanes and hedge-rows can assume.[77]

From the beginning, Parents' Review articles and P.N.E.U. programs mention flower pressing and other collections. "To mount in scrap-book, six wild flowers, with leaves; to know their names, and whether they grow in field or hedge or marsh."[78] It is not evident whether this work always went into the Nature Notebook or if there were other collection methods. Occasionally we do find a pressed flower in the archived nature diaries, but since more than a few pressings would obviously make the books too thick, and classroom displays are mentioned, there were likely several ways to pursue this work. As *The Parents' Review* article below advises, Nature Notebooks and collections are made by students of all ages, as a way to foster observation.[79]

> Another faculty of the mind, which parents and teachers must develop in their children, is the power of observation; acquaintance with natural history and natural objects is an excellent manner of training the power of observation. The knowledge of natural phenomena must not be theoretical but wholly practical; the child must gain his knowledge independently, by personal experience. [80]

Collecting is less about amassing finds than ensuring this personal connection. This is supported by bringing together likeminded friends and useful resources.

> The Union possesses a natural history club, from which each branch can receive pamphlets and books treating on nature lore and natural history. Some branches have their own natural history clubs, the work of which has proved very satisfactory. The club arranges rambles and excursions for its members on a systematic plan. It edits a journal called The Children's Quarterly.
>
> Every year, in May, during the annual conference, there is an exhibition of the works made by the young members of the club, which consist in collections of dried plants, drawings of flowers, plants and insects, which are often accompanied by personal descriptions, remarks and observations of the young explorer. Furthermore, it guides amateurs in giving Nature lessons, and recommends suitable

text-books bearing on each section of natural history that is being taken up. Let me read to you, from one of the Natural History Club pamphlets, some suggestions for children's work, Spring, 1899.

For Members over ten years—

"No. 1.—Make a list of the flowers in your garden, and another of the flowers you see in the hedges."

"No. 2.—Watch the leaf buds as they open from day to day, and make notes of anything that strikes you in their various methods of opening."

"No. 3—Make a list of the dates when the fruit trees blossom."

"No. 4.—Chrysalises collected in the autumn should be placed in dry moss in suitable breeding cages. Drawings should be made of them, and notes taken of their colour, structure, etc. Draw and describe the butterflies and moths that emerge."

For the children under ten the "suggestion" is:—

"Make sketches of six different kinds of spring flowers, and tell where you found the flower and when. Don't forget the leaves."

…last year, during the summer vacation, an experiment was made by some members of the Union to awaken the interest in Nature studies amongst the children of the poorer classes. For a beginning the result proved satisfactory.[81]

I have quoted this interesting passage at length since several things emerge worth noting: one, even though the children's Nature Notebooks were interest-led and "left up to them," there are practical, age appropriate suggestions made by the adults involved on how to use them, at least in the Natural History Clubs; two, there is an atmosphere or culture of interest created by the branches (parents) to provide scaffolding in the form of excursions, meetings, materials, and teacher training; and three, there is an impetus to awaken this interest in others of lesser means, which seems to be a signature of Mason's educational revolution—access for all children. Here then are intentional practices that go far beyond simply providing students a notebook and some paints.[82]

Family Diary

The Family Diary is another notebook mentioned in passing: "there is no end of things to be seen and noted. The party come across a big tree which they judge, from its build, to be an oak—down it goes into the diary."[83] Since it appears in a long passage about life out-of-doors and outings, and is found in *Home Education* which addresses the care of children under nine and in the home, we assume Mason means that mothers keep a family record to model the practice until the small children "are able" to keep their own Nature Notebooks. It could also be a compilation of all the family's nature knowledge was wanted, just as the schools made compilations from the individual students' records.[84]

Science Notebooks/ Lab Books

How these studies became more systematic science researches is a typical question for readers and not explicitly spelled out; did Mason's students eventually keep lab books as we understand them today? In the upper forms (IV and V) a syllabus reads, "Specimens should be used in all botanical work, and experiments must be made. Keep a Nature Note-Book. Choose special studies."[85] Since experiments are mentioned right alongside the instructions for nature studies it may be that the Nature Notebook's "catholicity" extended even to the formal recording of experiments. Possibly the poetic study of science Mason called for was not quite so compartmentalized as we have it today.[86] Instead of separate lab books for each science discipline, perhaps Biology and Astronomy continue to be at home together, and perhaps even Physics demonstrations are sought in the natural world and written up in the Nature Notebook. More research may tell. There are science notebooks present in the Mason archive wherein House of Education students recorded notes on all different science topics within one cover, simply dating the page and adding the appropriate headings, "Botany," "Astronomy," and even "Architecture," and presumably these teachers in training would have set up their upper year students in the same integrated manner.[87]

Calendar of Firsts

Also associated with the Nature Notebook is what Mason refers to as "a Calendar of Firsts."

It is a capital plan for children to keep a calendar—the first oak leaf, the first tadpole, the first cowslip, the first catkin, the first ripe blackberries, where seen and when. The next year they will know when and where to look out for their favourites, and will, every year, be in a condition to add new observations. Think of the zest and interest, the *object*, which such a practice will give to daily walks and little excursions. There is hardly a day when some friend may not be expected to hold a first "At Home."[88]

Specifics about how this calendar is to be set up are not given. There is some evidence that the Calendar was not distinct from the Nature Notebook; there are examples in the archive of Nature Notebooks containing a single page with a heading "Spring 19—" and a dated listing of firsts of that year's spring. (fig.3) Yet in order to see differences by year there is a clear benefit to not having entries buried within one's Nature Notebook but recorded year on year in a single volume, a Book of Firsts. Any "Book of Days" or perpetual calendar (i.e. a datebook with no year indicated as in figure 4) in which one can add first sightings can serve the purpose.[89] It is clear that the very youngest children were participating in this kind of noticing, and we can assume that it became a lifelong habit. Similar to the recording eventually needed to make the life lists of birds, insects, and plants described above, the Book of Firsts, as it has come to be known in this century, may scaffold the more involved lists to come.

Spring 2011
Birdsong in bright 10 am sunshine Feb. 23
Light till 6 p.m. Mar. 1
Fat robin- Mar. 7 in a snow and ice storm
50's and heavy rain Mar. 11
geese and chipmunks return Mar. 12
temps in the 70's Mar. 18
snowdrops Mar.23
tips of Daff's Mar. 29
snow! Nor'Easter, Apr. 1
Frost! Apr. 6

Fig. 3 Calendar of Firsts *(design Laurie Bestvater)*

January		
25		
26		
27 flock of robins, 15 or more, eating service berries 2010 Blizzard 2011		
28		
29 mild, 40F, first squirrels 2008		
30		

Fig. 4 Book of Firsts *(design Laurie Bestvater)*

Copybooks

Another familiar notebook Mason relies on is known as the Copybook. In the 19th century, copybooks were typically the means for early printing lessons through copying the "proverbs or maxims, extolling virtues such as honesty or fair dealing that were printed at the top of the pages….The school-children had to write them by hand repeatedly down the page."[90]

We have a clue to Mason's opinion of this moralistic practice in her response to Mrs. Bridges' "system of beautiful handwriting…. We have waited patiently, though not without some urgency, for the production of this new kind of copy-book."[91] Bridges allowed Mason to move her pupils away from the endless copying of the same motto all down the page in a utilitarian script which she felt was monotonous for the students and did not lead to a good hand (nor, likely, moral rectitude). The "plates" included in Bridges' "new system" allowed the student to move to the blackboard and slate to learn the stroke of the beautiful letter and thus erase it quickly if an error was made before ever trying to copy a perfect set of letters or a whole motto. The combination of this inspiring script and eliminating "set headlines" liberated the Copybook to become individualized and much more interesting and, hence, effective.[92] Students would still be instructed by the slow copying of beautiful lines but, characteristic of Mason, the words would be the ones that spoke to their hearts, or at least be words with a context—coming from their readings.

Poetry Book

Thus, the first "copybook" might be a collection of a student's favorite verses of poetry. Mason suggests enhancing the children's relationship with the text and strengthening their penmanship simultaneously with a primary Poetry Book.

> Children should transcribe favourite passages—a certain sense of possession and delight may be added to this exercise if children are allowed to choose for transcription their favourite verse in one poem and another. This is better than to write a favourite poem, an exercise that stales on the little people before it is finished. But a book of their own made up of their own chosen verses, should give them pleasure.[93]

Children in the Parents' Union Schools continued to copy in various ways throughout their school years, observing the aptness of words, the beauty of the script, the style of the great writers, and the largesse of ideas in such copybooks.

Motto Books/ Student Year-book

Thus Mason's copybooks have an array of permutations: there is mention of a Motto Book or Student Year-book, allowing copybook principles to be upheld with creativity and variety.[94] Mason feels that moral impetus has to come from an idea striking the child and that "the culling" is the most important and personal feature of the activity.

> In the reading of the Bible, of poetry, of the best prose, the culling of mottos is a delightful and most stimulating occupation, especially if a motto book be kept, perhaps under headings, perhaps not. It would not be a bad idea for children to make their own year-book, with a motto for every day in the year culled from their own reading. What an incentive to a good day it would be to read in the morning as a motto of our very own choice and selection,

and not the voice of an outside mentor: "keep ye the law; be swift in all obedience!" The theme suggests endless subjects for consideration and direct teaching; for example, lives with a keynote; Bible heroes; Greek heroes; poems of moral inspiration; poems of patriotism, duty, or any single moral quality; moral object lessons; mottoes and where to find them, etc.[95]

Beautiful script is also a value in itself; Sundays were often spent by P.N.E.U. students working on a beautiful rendition of a particular passage on fine paper.[96] Perhaps these were even illuminated, as was the fashion at the time.[97] And we have seen how beginning writers use copy work, in part to strengthen penmanship skills, but Mason is also after something more meditative and formative here. Why else would her students sometimes copy a whole book of the Gospel?[98] This is not busywork; rather it is an intentional practice with much more profound implications. Mason sees the spark needed for moral behavior comes to the students not in lectures from the Head of School, admonitions from the pulpit, or from posters advertising the character trait of the week, but from an inspiring character in their novel or a brief line in a poem. As an idea is spiritual, it needs a place to intersect with the student's own spirit, in this case, in the slowly emerging text of the meditative copy work.

In her essay, "The Writer's Notebook," American poet Luci Shaw refers to the hidden treasures of such reflective writing, a thought that applies to Mason's deep reliance on meditation—taking time to write by hand slows us down and allows truth to seep in.[99]

> Though we are often moving too fast to notice it, there is in each of us a profound need to be still, to be alone, to reflect, to meditate, to contemplate, to wait to reach a kind of bone-deep honesty with our own souls. Keeping a reflective journal (or copybook -Ed.) takes time, which is a valuable commodity for all of us. The time taken enhances this learning. It compels us to slow down, to decelerate. I like the word *cognition*. It means "shaking together," which is what our minds do with the thoughts that come and go, given time. A kind of cerebral ballet is performed within our minds if we allow ourselves time to focus and to be disciplined.

This slowing down also allows us to pay attention. *Ad-tendre* is the Latin verb "to reach toward." The more I use my journal as a collection jar for my writing, the more I find myself developing the habit of intentionally noticing things—objects, facts, experiences.[100]

So copying from the rich banquet Mason spreads through all the "subjects" is much more than an efficient method of teaching handwriting; it is a daily posture of reception and response. This "cerebral ballet" is one of the forms of self-activity that Mason relies on, and it turns up all through the day. For example, relevant bits of verse might be copied into the nature notebook; a quote on citizenship might appear in the Calendar of Events; a folksong is copied into a history narration, and so on.

Fortitude Journal

A copybook might also be specially pressed into service to offer support for an individual child's most tenacious character challenge. If selected by the child and not coming from an external judge, this habit of noticing passages on a particular trait the child has identified as wanting to strengthen can be deeply inspiring and formative. One example of this type of book mentioned by Mason, almost off the cuff, in conjunction with the book *Ourselves* and the painting by Botticelli,[101] is the Fortitude Journal:

> Instead of gradually ascending, we have come down from the high ideal of Fortitude to commonplace, even absurd, examples; but these fit our occasions; and it would not be a bad plan to keep a note-book recording the persons and incidents that give a fillip to conscience in this matter of fortitude.[102]

A fillip is that quick flick which every child knows and Webster describes as that "strike with the nail of the finger, first placed against the ball of the thumb, and forced from that position with some violence."[103] So this kind of (specialized) copybook is created based on whatever is tweaking us! It would be of no use to have every student produce a Fortitude Journal, no matter how the teacher felt it a problem in her day, if the student himself did not identify it as his own besetting issue. One student could choose to keep a "Gratitude Journal," another may want to collect passages on kindness.[104] The fact that Mason suggests it offhand with "it might not be a bad idea," shows her wisdom; she is reminding us that we must not "point the moral."[105] This type of notebook is gently suggested as an aid to have up our sleeves, so to speak, in the case of such a delicate instance. The possibilities for abuse in this idea are apparent; a teacher or parent identifying a character trait a child needs to "fix" and assigning a notebook on the topic is an impertinent prospect.

As Shaw remarks, keeping such a journal has its own formative effect.

> Call it serendipity, but if our ears and eyes are open to the vast world of events and ideas, we will find that what we need is available. I call this mechanism the writer's or the artist's antenna. And our recording device, our handy journal, allows us to capture this fleeting idea and pin it to the page.[106]

This is not a practice for young children. The Fortitude Journal is suggested in *Ourselves* Book II, which is written for "older students of life," age 16 and up. So keeping this kind of focused copybook likely progressed from the making of poetry collections and motto books in the younger years and moved to serious notice of spiritual formation in the upper, alongside the reading and discussion of *Ourselves* and the spiritual practices of the Church such as Catechism instruction and Confirmation of Baptism.[107]

Commonplace Book

If a notebook like the Fortitude Journal is the microscope of copybooks, then the Commonplace Book is the wide-angle lens. Like the Nature Notebook, it could also be described, as "very catholic" while the Fortitude Journal is obviously specific. The Commonplace collects student-selected passages but from any and all reading on any and all subjects. Mason also refers to it as a Reading Diary. Though a Commonplace may contain student writing in the form of the odd character sketch or plot summary, it generally consists of other people's writing. Like a graduated form of the copybook, it is begun in earnest by the student at middle or high school age when his learning is becoming more and more under his own direction and, ideally, used throughout life.[108]

> It is very helpful to read with a commonplace book or reading-diary, in which to put down any striking thought in your author, or your own impression of the work, or any part of it; but not summaries of facts….we never forget the book that we have made extracts from, and of which we have taken the trouble to write a short review.[109]

As noted in the first chapter, drawing on a practice in deep use by European and North American scholars wherein proverbial wisdom and passages from the reading of academic subjects were collected, the syllabus instructs Form IV to "keep a Commonplace Book for passages that strike you particularly"[110]And likely, the students would have known exactly what was meant: a personalized notebook that crossed subjects and was meant to go with them everywhere as a dear companion and a record of their reading/learning.[111]

Other "Copybooks"

Beyond the learning to write, collection of beautiful passages, and usefulness for acquiring habits, there is also a more universal use of the term copybook to consider: was "copybook" used interchangeably with notebook or exercise book? For example, archives show George Washington's "copybooks"—separate notebooks for "Math," "Poetry," and "Gentlemanly Behaviour" from the time he was a teen, 1743-45.[112] In the 1800's it was typically still copying the work of the masters, not original any more than a geometry solution is original. Later P.N.E.U. programs record that "exercise books with the motto and crest printed on them" were for sale from the P.N.E.U. offices, leading one to wonder if Charlotte Mason's students might also have compiled such books by subject.[113] Unfortunately, there is little said about where the daily written narrations were kept, presumably in such exercise books but perhaps even on loose leaf. Teachers have had to solve for themselves, keeping Mason's principles in mind, whether narrations should be divided by subject, if copy work is included in the same notebook or kept separate, and other such niggling classroom matters.

Music

Music copybooks are just such an example. While we do not know for certain that Mason's students kept separate music copybooks, we do have references to students copying music in *Home Education*[114] and in upper level exams: "Write three lines from any five of the following:—Joseph Joachim, Johann Strauss the younger, the 'Sos(?)atensatz,' 'Marxsen', the two versions of the 'Waltzes,' Brahms' treatment of German folk song 'Remenyi.'"[115] So it is conceivable that students were keeping music copybooks. Did the copybook expand to include narrations of a musician's life? Or did the life show up on a century chart and in the Book of Centuries? The answer is likely, "yes and yes."[116]

Travel Diary

We know only that Mason kept these herself, resulting in *The Forty Shires* and *The Ambleside Geographies*. Presumably, Geography that "takes the child there," would require a similar kind of approach, but Nature Notebooks also traveled so it seems that the practice of noticing and narrating is again more important than the specific notebook chosen.

Bible Notebook

Mason also makes a brief mention of a notebook in connection with the study of the scriptures, likely kept for narrations and perhaps maps and copy work: "Let us observe, notebook in hand, the orderly and progressive sequence, the penetrating quality, the irresistible appeal, the unique content of the Divine teaching."[117] Again, there is little certainty; given Mason's sacramental approach to life, one could conceive of all of the notebooks within this brief description.

My Word Book

There is another category of notebook—those used for short periods of time by the adults in the child's life to scaffold their learning. The delightful

Word Book is one such: "Tommy's new words (from his nursery rhyme reading) are written (by the teacher) in his 'note-book' in print hand, so that he can take stock of his possessions in the way of words."[118] These are words he knows "like the face of a friend in a crowd of strangers, and he is able to pounce upon (them) anywhere." The parent or teacher keeps this notebook *for* the prewriting child in a supportive and loving way to celebrate with him, as he begins to break the code of the printed world, that "already (he) has accumulated a little capital."[119]

French Notebook

Similarly, a notebook is used to scaffold the unfolding second language; again, *the teacher* keeps it. The idea is for the teacher to have a record of the words and phrases the child is using consistently so to adjust the teaching.[120] Since a native speaker (baby) hears his language for several years before becoming aware of print, so the student would not see this French notebook or the written word, at least not at first. It is not clear whether or not the student might take over this notebook to have it function much as the Word Book does in his English reading when he begins written work in the second language at about year 4, but it seems a useful and consistent idea. Likewise, there is no reason to think that a similar book would not be kept for each of the other languages taught under this method, with a similar progression, i.e. from oral scaffolding to the printed word.[121]

Parent Year-book

"Is Edward a selfish child when his fifth birthday comes? The fact is noted in his parents' year-book, with the resolve that by his sixth birthday he shall, please God, be a generous child."[122] This is another interesting notebook. There is only the one reference, but it is significant in its suggestion of proactive parenting and habit training based on observation and respect.[123] A permutation based on the close observation of children may allow keeping such a notebook to become a helpful practice within a school community— the parents doing such an assessment of their child to share with the teachers and vice versa so that there is a thoughtful conversation amongst the adults governing the child's education. (Exactly how to be rid of selfishness in one year is not explained, however.)[124] As writing about "Edward's selfishness" no doubt involves consideration of the parents' own behavior and aims, the idea of the "Parent Year-book" might also suggest a tool for the self-reflection of teachers—particular journaling about their teaching.

Way of the Will Chart/Map of Mansoul

Though the Way of the Will and the geography of Mansoul are topics suggested for middle to upper school ages as a very important area of focus, it is doubtful that Mason refers to an actual chart or map here. It is clear that in the interest of forming self-awareness, developing character and an informed conscience, Mason consistently and consciously prepares a rich banquet meant to feed the child's understanding of "the Way of the Will"— what it means to be human and to choose. "There is no occasion to panic, but it is time that we realised that to fortify the will is one of the great purposes of education, and probably some study of the map of the City of Mansoul would afford us guidance.[125] Though her whole methodology and curriculum are put to the purpose, the "map" is metaphorical and she refers to it in the first half of her unique book *Ourselves* designed to be read through slowly with students ages 12-16 as they discover and name the things that make them human beings—to provide a "carefully considered ground plan of human nature."[126] I am imaging here a project undertaken upon the reading of the first book of *Ourselves,* wherein students design an artistic or visual narration—their own map of Mansoul.[127]

> In his history lessons and his reading of tale and poem, he comes across persons each of whom carries his point by strong wilfulness [sic]. He laughs at that rash boy Phaeton...and through this and many other examples, recognizes that a strong will is not synonymous with "being good" nor with a determination to have your own way. He learns to distribute the characters he comes across in his reading on either side of a line, those who are wilful and those who are governed by will; and this line by no means separates between the bad and the good.[128]

The Way of the Will Chart is similar; Mason probably envisions this only symbolically—as a mental dividing line—but an actual "Way of the Will Chart" based on her description proves a useful tool to help explain the concept to teachers and upper year students who are reading book two of *Ourselves.*[129] The chart is useful across the subjects but especially in Literature and History if, for a short time, students put characters (real or fictional) on the proper side of the line in a conscious way. Once they recognize the difference between choosing/willing and what Mason calls "willfulness," the chart has served its purpose and can be referenced mentally in further discussions. Mason wants it to dawn on her student that living by willfulness, going along with the crowd or our own impulses, is not really living at all, that it is in choosing that we are most fully human. Metaphorical or actual, the chart also helps students to notice that a person does not consistently fit on one side of the line or the other, and that even acts of choice can have evil or good outcomes.

"The Enquire Within" or Household Book

> May I suggest the great use and value of a household book, in which the young housekeeper notes down exactly how to do everything, from the scouring of a floor to the making of an omelet, either as she has done it herself, or has watched it being done, with the little special wrinkles that every household gathers. Such an "Enquire Within" should be invaluable hereafter, as containing personal experiences, and should enable her to speak with authority to cook or housemaid who "Never saw it done like that, ma'am."[130]

Mason's reference to the Enquire Within refers to an actual Victorian phenomenon published first in 1856 called "The Enquire Within Upon Everything." It included etiquette, parlor games, recipes, laundry tips, holiday preparation ideas, and first aid among other things. It ran one hundred thirteen editions and was last printed in 1976.[131] It was what the title implied, a place to find everything from detailed entries about the rules of Croquet to short form instructions for a particular crochet stitch. It is not surprising that the inventor of the World Wide Web considered the name, "The Enquire Within," since the volumes were essentially the Victorian equivalent of "Google."[132]

What Mason envisions is not strictly a copybook, more like a collection of specific, practical narrations. Besides the "Nursery Book," which the participants in the Mothers' Reading Course were entreated to make, The Enquire Within stands by itself within Mason's collection of notebooks in encouraging an "instruction sheet" type of narration—the beginning of the form known as a process essay, that is, "tell how to do X."[133] Of course, originally, the book was suggested for young ladies who would be more than likely to take over great houses with great housekeeping duties, but the notion could be applied to any student endeavor based on interest, personal observation, and experience. Household maintenance and gardening, for example, were included and are just as useful to students today. Perhaps all the student's handicraft, art, and practical subjects, almost any topic of concern, could be recorded here as a collection of useful things one wants to remember. Again, what one can tell, one knows. What one cannot tell, one does not know.

Timelines, History Charts and Book of Centuries

Think back to your childhood history education. What did you learn and how did you learn it? What stuck with you? If asked right now, could you sketch a basic outline of history? Get a list of events in relatively the right order? Most adults, when asked, giggle nervously and hope these questions are some kind of joke or party game. If pressed, they admit that their schooling in history was miserably inadequate—a hodgepodge of often repeated topics or largely a dark question mark. After the relief of finding I am not really looking for an answer, most are excited to hear of Mason's clever and effective way of supporting a child's history learning: the Book of Centuries developed by Mrs. Bernau and promoted in the Parents' Union Schools.

Writing to possible skeptics in a booklet called "P.N.E.U. Methods of Teaching," Mr. Household, Mason's longtime advocate and Secretary for Education, Gloucestershire, writes bemusedly, "Believe in this, as in other things, that what Charlotte Mason says the child will do, *do* it surely will. Have Faith."[134] As many readers of Mason will attest, it often takes too long to find this out: "there is no part of a child's work at school which some philosophic principle does not underlie," the implication being, in which case, one thing is *not* as good as another.[135] Household is a convert: if Mason says it or does it, there is a specific reason. Looking at her pedagogy closely, one does not see a cobbled together educational grab-bag but a cohesive philosophy, a unity generating an elegant method that supports human learning in the most profound ways. In passing seemingly unimportant phrases in her works or in reading others *about her* rather than Mason herself, real treasures have been missed—the Book of Centuries is a case in point. One may read many times in the programs that children are "to keep a Book of Centuries" but be content to take definitions wrought by others, as I did, rather than follow the trail through her writings to discover exactly what Mason meant by a Book of Centuries. What has been misinterpreted as essentially a timeline compressed into a book is actually so much more.

One of Mason's primary purposes for making history the "pivot" of her curriculum is to allow the child see the flow of history and to think of himself within it.[136]

> Once Intellect admits us into the realms of History, we live in a great and stirring world, full of entertainment and sometimes of regret; and at last we begin to understand that we too are making History, and *that we are all part of the whole;* that the people who went before us were all very like ourselves, or else we should not be able to understand them. If some of them were worse than we and in some things their times were worse than ours, yet we make acquaintance with *many who were noble and great, and our hearts beat with a desire to be like them.*[137] (emphasis mine)

To help children keep this flow of history in view, Mason uses a variety of what I call time tools and we must back up and look at these before the Book of Centuries can be seen in its proper context as the remarkable pillar of her method that it is. Mason does indeed recommend using timelines, but it takes some sleuthing to uncover that she refers to more than one version and each has its own purposes and limitations. Here is what she says about one of the first steps.

Table of History

> In order to give definiteness to what may soon become a pretty wide knowledge of history—mount a sheet of cartridge paper and divide it into twenty columns, letting the first century of the Christian era come in the middle, and let each remaining column represent a century B.C. or A.D. as the case may be. Then let the child himself write or print, as he is able, the names of the people he comes

1000	900	800	700	600	500	400	300	200	100 BC	100 AD	200	300	400	500	600	700	800	900	1000
HOMER						ALEXANDER			CAESAR	JESUS		CONSTANTINE					CHARLEMAGNE	ALFRED	

Fig. 5 "Table of the Centuries" *(design Laurie Bestvater)*

upon in due order, in their proper century. We need not trouble ourselves *at present* with more exact dates, but this simple table of the centuries will suggest *a graphic panorama* to the child's mind, and he will see events in their time-order.[138] (emphasis mine)

There are several things to notice in this passage. First, that this timeline is not very big—one sheet of paper.[139] Second, it is very simple, twenty columns representing only twenty centuries both A.D. and B.C. and not all of recorded time. The names selected were particular to the child's reading and it is enough, at this point, to sort them generally by century and not by year. It is described as "graphic," and "mounted," which means the timeline is kept visible for creating a basic time sense and likely not part of a book but a small, easily-referenced poster, something mounted on the wall—possibly like the simple, compact, child-oriented version depicted above. (fig.5)

I have regarded this "Table of the Centuries" as elementary because the reference comes from *Home Education* which addresses the needs of children under nine. Also, the limit of twenty centuries, ten on each side of the birth of Christ suggests the hero tales and ancients that were typically scheduled for the younger children in Mason's scope and sequence.[140] So, while we do not know exactly when Mason is using a timeline like this, it would have to be with young children, evidenced also by the phrase "what will soon become." Mason is not as concerned in the earliest years with chronology. As Nesbitt explains, "lists of names and dates to be learned by heart may have their place, but they are the dry bones of history, a firm and necessary skeleton, but to be studied after, and not before, the human form."[141] So, The Table of History is likely used at the end of Form I or part of Form II with the definite beginning of a chronological study of history.

History/Century Charts

Distinct from the Table of History, History Charts are noted in *Towards a Philosophy of Education* and in many other P.N.E.U. writings and programs. "Pupils make history charts for every hundred years on the plan either adapted or invented by the late Miss Beale of Cheltenham, a square ruled into a hundred spaces, ten in each direction, with the symbol in each square showing an event."[142] Mason obviously admires and adopts these History, sometimes called Century, charts. Based on Beale's article, "The Teaching of Chronology," we can see that as early as 1891 she recommends these mnemonic time grids for students in Form III and on.[143] The hundred squares represent, roughly, the length of a man's life or a century, the first upper left hand square standing for zero, the last, lower right-hand square becoming 99 in that century. This made History charts a practical and very symbolic ("hieroglyphic") way to locate and record Mason's program of chronological reading through Science, History, Literature, poetry, or what have you.

Beale is clear on the advantages of such a tool:

1. That it forms a framework, which from the first saves events from getting shaken into disorder in the memory, and the frame can be made large or small, filled but scantily at first and gradually expanded.
2. It can be adapted to any purpose—political history, church history, literary history, the progress of scientific discovery.
3. It shows at a glance the contemporary history of different countries yet
4. It is compact in form, so that it can be easily remembered.
5. Even if the precise date of any event is not retained, yet the general position becomes as familiar to the mind as the relative positions of places in a map of Europe.[144]

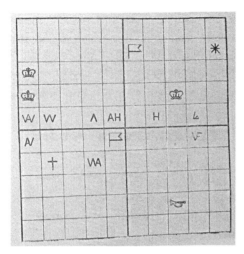

Fig.6. Beale's History Chart (also known as Century Chart)[146] *(Image used under license from the Charlotte Mason Digital Collection, Redeemer University College, Ancaster, Ontario, Canada.)*

R.A. Pennethorne, student of the House of Education, describes the mnemonic effect of these Century Charts, indeed, the personal connections shaped by all of Mason's time tools, as helping "the children to get a grip of the world's progress from Alexander the Great to the Right Hon. Cecil Rhodes, as a Catholic comprehends his whole faith by the beads on his rosary" i.e. these History/Century Charts are symbolic and representational aids to memory.[145]

Other Steps

Apart from the Book of Centuries then, the Table of History and the History/Centuries Charts are the only time tools we know for certain Mason recommends. And they are very different sorts of scaffolding, seemingly at two ends of the spectrum: the one very simple for beginning students and the other, abstract and symbolic for the older. Were there other steps? Mason only hints at this as she describes the Table of History, with the phrase, "We need not trouble ourselves *at present* with more exact dates," which I take to suggest that something more complex was to come.[146] There are references to other time tools in *The Parents' Review*. "The Teaching of History" written by an H.B. in 1894, and Miss Beale's 1891 article, "The Teaching of

Chronology,"[147] both describe something a bit more complex than Mason's two steps in building the history scaffolding.[148] Since she was editing *The Parents' Review* at the time of publication and since she admired Beale's method elsewhere, where these articles agree with each other and Mason's principles, I assume these other time tools were being used in P.N.E.U. classrooms and homes.[149]

As I have tried to piece together the places where Beale and H.B. agree, many of Mason's principles emerge. For example, H.B. echoes Mason's perennial emphasis on seeing and on livingness.[150]

> To present historical events *to the eye* even thus imperfectly, as will be evident to every educationist, is a large step towards rendering history something more than a mere loose chain of isolated events, and to make it more easy to introduce something of *organic life* into the often some- what vague and mechanical conception produced in the mind of the learner by the ordinary teaching of elementary history.[151] (emphasis mine)

Most importantly, H.B. and Beale concur that there are three basic steps in the construction of the child's time sense and discuss corresponding tools, which I name, again attempting clarity: The Child's Own History, The Bird's Eye Views, and Close Quarters tools.[152]

The chart below (fig.7) is an overview of these three platforms. The time tools we know Mason recommended herself are indicated. I follow the chart with specific descriptions for each of the conjectured steps since the use of a variety of names within the P.N.E.U creates some confusion. Mason's signature, and the thing to note that we find with these "other steps," is although they are different activities, they all take the child from the known to the unknown—from the "present (as) our starting point" and personal, to a macro view and only then to the specialized or micro view of the mature history student.[153] Here too, as in the whole of her curriculum, Mason's design allows for "scaffolding"—for knowledge to be built up slowly, with the child's own connections lending the next hand-hold to new knowledge.

(under 6/7)	Child's Own (Form I as ready)	Bird's Eye Views (Forms II & III as ready)		Close Quarters (Form III & up)
No time tools used	create a visible chart in 3 month divisions	Chronological study of History begun Continue to create an idea of a century Move from "Table of History"* to "Stream of History"		History/Century charts of a special period*
complete idea of time not evident yet	From present into past in stages			mind and study tool
				Increasingly symbolic/ mnemonic
Gathering tales, the heroic, vivid pictures & things *in situ*	1. his life, sibs, birthdays, holidays	1. Table of History* Persons entered as he comes upon them Drawn for himself	2. "Stream of History" Condensed (yard= 3000 yrs.) Essential facts only Visible as a whole by decade One's own country predominate	Breakout Hooks to "the Stream of History" which continues to be added to
	2. add local events			Useful in Science, Music, Literature, etc.
	build a notion of a century			
		Book of Centuries * started **in Form II continues**		

Fig.7: Mason's Time Scaffolding *specified by Mason *(design Laurie Bestvater)*

The Child's Own History

As we know, the young child has very little time sense, often charmingly mixing up the words for yesterday and tomorrow. By age seven or eight, it is clearer to him that things have happened before his time and the child goes on to develop the notion of a century, and only after that the vastness of all recorded history and prehistory. We have seen that Mason waits for this dawning to attempt the narrowing to specific dates and events because of her characteristic sympathy with the child. "As for the dates, they never come right; the tens and units he can get, but the centuries will go astray; and how is he to put the right events in the right reign, when to him, one king differs from another only in number, one period from another only in date?"[154]

Accordingly then, coming before or perhaps overlapping somewhat, Mason's Table of History, it seems the first tool recommended is the Child's Own History Chart (fig.8). Specific guidelines are given in "History: Teaching Practically Considered" for making this chart starting whenever the child appears ready. It starts with the present, adding perhaps only the child's last birthday as a first entry. And then all his birthdays added in other sessions as far back as he can remember and to his birth.

The child may remember the birth of a sibling so that is the next layer of history added. Soon, family events like remarkable holidays or ceremonies

	1990	1991	1992	1993	1994	1995	1996	1997	1998
My Birthdays		Me!	1	2	3	4	5	6	7
Sarah	4 JK	5	6	7	8	9	10	11	12
Caleb							1	2	3
Family		Windermere PastorPoppa		Reunion Jetta	Our dog Wesley		40th Ann.		Korea
Holidays				Germany Florida	Eganville	"Phantom" Niagara Falls	Traverse City		East Lawn Bali
Public	Hubble Telescope	Gulf War		Prime Min. Chretien					

Fig.8. Model for Child's Own History Chart *(design Laurie Bestvater)*

are included and only when the habit of thinking historically becomes clear to the child are public events noted, working from a local event like a parade or fair he participated in. Finally, the national events within his own time like elections or noted discoveries are included. It is only after this history is solidly understood that events in "Grandpa's time" can be examined until the child has a fairly complete notion of his century.[155]

This unfolding may take only a short time for the child who is ready, but H.B. envisioned The Child's Own History chart as coming about gradually, as a special family activity. Something framed in the way of a "sampler" is suggested, dividing each year into three terms is another possibility. Beale prefers using symbols, a ship telling of a journey and such like; there are probably many ways to create such a cherished record for the child that awakens interest and is highly personalized just so long as it is not enclosed in a book. The chart needs to be highly visible, a type of wall art. Both authors have the overarching idea of building knowledge by the student's own connections which we scaffold in this delightful way until he knows there were other times before this one, (Long, Long Ago and Far, Far, Away). I have a history; everyone has a history. I fit into a larger history (families make up public life). A hundred years is a century.

The value of this practice may be much greater than the simple primary activity it first appears to be. Educational critic Thomas Armstrong notices a similar practice in *The Best Schools*. Even the older students at Web Middle School in Austin, Texas, found great value in creating such a "life graph."[156] One can only wonder at the effect of this process when combined with Mason's consecutive reading of History.

Birds Eye Views

1. Table of History/Map of Centuries
With the notion of a century secure, perhaps coincident with the child's conception of a hundred chart, next the child is helped to know that centuries make up all of time and that there were certain qualities and happenings of particular times. Beale puts it like this:

> But when one century has been thus treated, I would place before the child a map, in which the eighteen Christian centuries are brought together thus on a small scale with some characteristic to give it individuality.[157]

1st Christianity	2nd Good Emperors	3rd Military despotism	4th Constantine	5th Fall of Rome
6th Barbaric Wars	7th Mahomet	8th Charlemagne	9th Alfred	10th Feudalism
11th Hildebrand	12th Crusades	13th Schoolmen	14th Rise of Middle-class	15th Renaissance
16th Reformation	17th Religious Wars	18th Political Wars	19th Revolution	20th

Fig. 9 Map of Centuries *(Image used under license from the Charlotte Mason Digital Collection, Redeemer University College, Ancaster, Ontario, Canada.)*

This "map" (fig.9) does relatively the same thing as Mason's Table of History (fig.3)—it quickly gives a sense that there are so many centuries and certain persons were living in them just as I am living in mine.[158] Both are visual maps of time, small enough to be taken in all at once and meant to include personal connections from the child's own reading. It is not clear if Beale's and the one Mason describes are one and the same or different and to be used in a particular order or both at the same time. Likely it is not important to know; they are both available to the child's growing time sense and the knowing teacher will refer to them as necessary and have them visible in the classroom.

2. Stream of History

Still under my heading "Bird's Eye Views," comes the next rung, a more complex time tool referred to by H.B. as encompassing the "stream of history."[159] The practice is confirmed by Beale: "Later, we should make such a chart on a larger scale, and with room for ruling and marking important events, we use charts coloured for various periods of English History."[160] "Next" and "later" do not do much to define when this more complex timeline was introduced. There is a slight reference by Mason: "Form IV is introduced to outlines of European history. The British Museum for Children and *Book of Centuries* are continued," which could refer to the start of this more intricate timeline.[161]

Beale is very specific about how it is to be done:

> On such a scale periods of ten years can be distinctly differentiated, while definite years may be clearly selected with care—key facts to the history of the time in which they occur, selected also in a catholic spirit, to represent without bias, the real historical weight of the various political forces, which in order to serve their purpose of historical landmarks, should already, before being introduced upon the chart, have been thoroughly familiar to the student.[162]

H.B. recommends a scale of 1000 years per foot—neither the round the classroom wall timeline, nor the compressed in a notebook type of timeline the current Mason community is accustomed to. This recommendation is again supporting all the Mason principles: flexible, student-produced, and personal, a time map of sorts. The articles concur on the extreme importance of it being visible "to the eye" and the primacy of the students' own connections, the timeline functioning as another type of narration—"a condensed chart representing the 3,000 years of history, during which the stream, which has now become the river of modern history, may be traced with some degree of definiteness towards its earliest sources. Such a chart might easily be condensed to such an extent as to be made conveniently visible as a whole, say within the compass of at most a yard in length."[163] We find almost the same thing being promoted by the P.N.E.U. in an undated publication by Winifred Irving called, "Notes on Making a Timeline."[164]

While more work needs to be done to discover all the possible iterations of P.N.E.U. "outlines", these documents do reveal that students are to be consistently supported along the way and are working up to a condensed timeline of particular features upholding Mason's principles of the livingness of their history study and the importance of the visual:

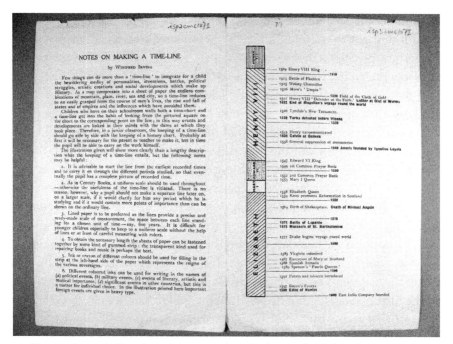

Fig.10. Irving's Timeline (*Image used under license from the Charlotte Mason Digital Collection, Redeemer University College, Ancaster, Ontario, Canada.*)

As a map compresses into a sheet of paper the endless combinations of mountain, plain, river, sea, and city, so a timeline reduces *to an easily grasped* form the course of men's lives, the rise and fall of states and of empires, and the influences which have moulded them. (my emphasis)[165]

Staying within the definition of "easily grasped," this timeline begins with the earliest times and new sheets are added (glued in) as study continues. It uses lined paper to create consistent units by decades; Irving calls anything less than uniform, "useless." It could be color coded but still relatively simple, containing only the "most important events." Again, this is not to say that there are no questions remaining about Mason's practice here, only that it seems very clear that there were definite things done for definite reasons consistent with the philosophy. Some have argued that there is no use in being a Mason purist, and I take the point. Likely any timeline is better than no timeline, but if Mason and the P.N.E.U. gave careful thought to scaffolding the child's growing time sense, are not some important principles at stake if we depart for the sake of convenience or personal preference for a less considered activity? For example, if the figures and dates are pre-printed or already selected for the child's insertion on a ready-made timeline, hasn't some mind other than the child's really done the connecting, selecting, and most of the sorting? It seems likely that there will be less attention and interest paid to this sort of timeline than to the personalized one Mason has envisioned, and hence less connection and retention. With a pre-printed or parent-chosen model, at best the child uses his scissor skills and finds the appropriate century to insert the cutout. Likewise, a classroom-sized timeline tracing the circumference of the room, while it upholds the mandate to keep the timeline a visible reference point, loses its condensed map-like impact. If a timeline only covers the history being studied that year in that particular classroom (taking part of the role of the history chart), it is a helpful tool but still manages to be less effective than what it seems the P.N.E.U. proposes. I am not suggesting we follow this rather involved trail just because it is the path Charlotte Mason trod; I hope I am presenting enough evidence to instigate a closer look at all her various practices in a search for the very good reasons underpinning them.

Close Quarters

Irving also refers to breakout charts of a more complex nature, like Beale's (fig. 5) History Charts that we explored earlier. The "Bird's Eye View" thus moves toward the more symbolic and specific Close Quarters examination as the older child makes a more in-depth descent into specific time periods. As is illustrated in the graphic below (fig.11), use of the more complex "Stream of History" continues, but History/Century charts allow for more detailed organization of the student's reading. For instance, if the year is spent reading in the 18th Century, a History Chart may be created for John Wesley or Peter the Great, Mozart or scientist Edward Jenner, creating a condensed and a visible order of a biography without clogging the time map that the Stream of History is meant to be. Like a blow-up of a city block or a diagram of a subway system, the close quarters tools work *with* the main map of the timeline, but do not replace it or take it over.

The terminology and the scant reference continue to be confusing. Like the Table of History and the Stream of History, there seem to be gradations of chart use, the teacher perhaps making the first basic model and moving to the older students ultimately adapting the template to their reading. It seems necessary to distinguish between Irving's "Time-line" as being a map of the whole of recorded history rather more like Beale's "Map of Centuries"(fig. 9), and the History/Century Charts Mason suggests the students make. Irving has also kept at least the "Stream of History" visible on the wall, and some version of the more compact, Close Quarters view, though unspecified: "Children who have on their schoolroom walls both a time chart and a time-line get into the habit of looking from the picture square on the chart to the corresponding point on the line; in this way, events and developments are linked in their minds with the dates at which they took place."[166]

Whatever remains unclear, it is evident (fig. 11) that these time tools flow and fit together, that they are not random but part of a very effective whole, and that over the child's entire school life they are available to build astounding support and cultivate a rather profound understanding of history. Mason's time scaffolding makes a sort of spiral progression not well depicted by the chart, from a child's own world, through a bird's eye overview, to the careful tracking of the flow of history and ultimately to the very specific details in the life of one man or one century of the serious student.

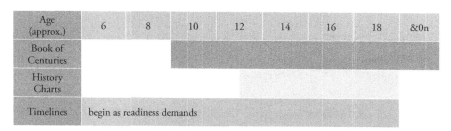

Figure 11: Mason's Use of Time Tools *(design Laurie Bestvater)*

The Book of Centuries

Thus is there a rather involved context for the Book of Centuries; while these time tools overlap and support each other, timelines, time charts, and Books of Centuries are separate things. Each has its own purposes and distinct parameters. It may help to think of them as "kissing cousins;" they are all of a family but with separate personalities and vocations.

So what is The Book of Centuries? It began as a museum notebook around 1906 and was essentially a sketchbook for drawing artifacts such as could be found in museums or from line drawings and photographs if a museum was out of reach. The practice originated out of Miss Bernau's relationship with Mrs. Epp who lived near the British Museum and taught her children Ancient History, especially with frequent museum visits. Bernau was herself a graduate of the House of Education, and with Mason's endorsement her notebook became by 1915 part of the P.N.E.U. program known as the Book of Centuries and eventually the P.N.E.U. office sold it as a specific design consisting of 96 pages, the cover embossed with the skylark emblem and motto: "I am, I can, I ought, I will."[167]

> The study of ancient history which cannot be contemporaneous we approach through a chronologically-arranged book about the British Museum…in which children draw such illustrations as they come across of objects of domestic use, of art, etc., connected with the century they are reading about. This slight study of the British Museum we find very valuable; whether the children have or have not the opportunity of visiting the Museum itself, they have the hope of doing so, and besides, their minds are awakened to the treasures of local museums.[168]

When a P.N.E.U program read "Keep a Book of Centuries putting in illustrations from all history studied,"[169] as Miss O'Farrell reveals, this meant that:

> In connection with this [reading the book *The British Museum for the Young]* each child keeps a century book, that is a large note book interleaved for drawing and writing, which they divide up, giving a page for each century back to about 15 B.C., earlier dates being added as required. In this book they draw specimens of the architecture, ancient implements, carvings, etc. of the period they are studying, and write in the names of famous people and events.[170]

The archive contains several of Bernau's descriptions of this simple Book of Centuries. Though some of them are undated, it is clear that she spoke about this particular time tool frequently over the years and though a few small details in its make-up and use changed, there was a very specific design given, based on and supporting the Ambleside method.[171]

Each two-page spread consists of a lined and a blank page and represents a century. The last 10 pages are kept for small drawings of maps and descriptions of history of the child's choice. The book begins with the prehistoric periods in a general way and runs chronologically through the present century. The entries on the lined pages are mainly events by date and selected by the child as "most characteristic" of that year. Pictures are rarely glued in—the value of the Book of Centuries is acknowledged as the careful observation and consideration required in drawing—also inserting pictures made the book too "bulky." The page opposing the drawing page has 20 lines in five (implied rather than demarcated) columns comprising 100 years, (an almost mnemonic chart much like Beal's use of one hundred spaces but not replacing those.) Entries are always done in Indian ink or a reasonable substitute with colors rarely, if ever, used.

The Book of Centuries takes time. It is not filled in all at once, even with a child studying one century at a time; it is a "life-long interest."[172] Bernau admits that she is dogmatic about its design and use:

> Naturally one page is a very small space in which to illustrate the whole of a century, and yet it is a mistake to leave two pages for some centuries, as I have seen in some books, *as it does away with the idea of the book*; therefore each should choose what she considers the most characteristic events, planning out the arrangement of the page, as far as possible, before drawing. In this way no two books will be alike, and there is great interest in comparing them.[173] (emphasis mine)

What a treasure Bernau's design is! It is so much simpler (and more elegant) and yet more structured than what has been typically understood in modern Mason circles and what I created with my first students—a big bulky timeline in a binder, a type of amalgam of the timeline/book of centuries that once begun was not easily redirected. Bernau's design has continued to surprise us; *"the idea"* of the book to which she refers is brilliant but easily missed. People are tempted to add pages in order to *cover* more. If the rows were wider, could we not fit in more? they wonder. Aware of

Mason's other time tools and applying her principles, we start to see why we would not want to do that: first, this is not about capturing all the history the child studies. The Book of Centuries is like a rope hammock: there are just enough points of contact to hold you up, but a lot of space too. This notebook is a visual touch point for the child, the century at a glance, personalized. It is a unique grid that testifies to an "imagination warmed," a mind map or filter for one's lifelong reading. If it has more than an hundred entries, Bernau argues, it becomes less effective and not more.[174]

The Book of Centuries is to history study what the Nature Notebook is to science: calling for focused observation and providing mental hooks, like Velcro. It is not meant to carry all the facts or personages the child encounters, just as the Nature notebook could never cover all of biology and natural history. It is designed to support sorting and relationship, connection, observation, and meditation. Like the Nature Notebook, each Book of Centuries is original and unique, the children choosing what is entered by their personal connection to the material. It is organic—"a live thing of present, past, and future," says Bernau, supporting the child's history understanding in a singular and vital way.[175]

Over and above the drawings proceeding from their general and ancient history work, children are encouraged to conduct a personal study of one particular thing or artifact and sketch it in the same place on each page of their notebook throughout the centuries. For example, early stringed instruments leading to an early violin and the modifications that ensued could be drawn if the child plays violin or an article of clothing that appeals, such as shoes or women's hats, is drawn from each century. Ships, weapons, cooking implements, the options for such a special study are as varied as the students.[176] Drawing the same thing, as it would be encountered in each century, provides that extra hook that once studied carefully enough to copy, belongs intimately to a student for the rest of his life.

This careful tracking and drawing of artifacts represents a practical outworking of Mason's pedagogy of books and things, left and right-brain education in balance. In the careful looking and drawing the child forms relationships in a different way than he does with the story or biography. Both sorts of relationships are enhanced and encompassed in the Book of Centuries' design. Thus the things as hooks for history knowledge go on one side of the notebook (the blank pages) and the ideas, events or personages read about, fill the hundred slots on the lined page opposite, resulting

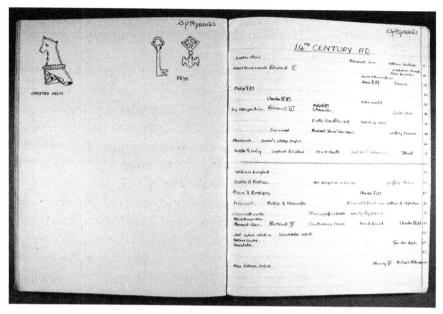

Fig. 12: Eve Anderson's Book of Centuries (*Image used under license from the Charlotte Mason Digital Collection, Redeemer University College, Ancaster, Ontario, Canada.*)

in the child's own history compendium. Bernau declares, "each book is an individual work of intelligence and, very often, art."[177]

Until recently, we had to take Bernau's word for it. With only a brief mention by Mason in the volumes to go on and the obscure imperative on the existing programs to "keep a Book of Centuries," we were bound to misunderstand. With the opening of the Charlotte Mason Digital Collection at Redeemer University College, we were permitted to see why Bernau called the Book of Centuries a "life-long" interest and "a great joy to the owner."[178] Eve Anderson, one of the last teachers trained in Mason's college, had donated her Book of Centuries to the archive and a picture is truly worth a thousand words.[179] The concept is really brilliant! Anderson's book (fig.12) confirms what Bernau consistently describes in several instances, a model adopted by the P.U.S. in 1915, with only minor adjustments: developments that offer very compelling reasons for Mason educators to adopt the actual Book of Centuries and not some other practice. My own use of this model has consistently revealed learning postures, new enthusiasms, and a fresh understanding of Mason's pedagogy. As the community gathered around Mason renews its serious use, I am convinced that the Book of Centuries will only grow in importance and indeed resume its esteemed and rightful place in a living education.

Reading Bernau in her later years, the impact of the Book of Centuries is apparent. It had become a beloved tradition. She recounts a charming story of children during WWI asking their Father who was home on leave and offering them a treat to go to the P.N.E.U. offices to purchase a ready-made Book of Centuries.[180] They wanted "the real thing," since they had been making do with exercise books in the economy of the Great War. She also describes having a "Book of Centuries Tea" with her students and those of Miss Kitching, where students would meet and enjoy each other's books and exchange illustrations for drawing much like children today might look forward to trading stickers or hockey cards. In London, there were "Book of Centuries Evenings," where Ambleside students would come and spend the evening drawing. Books of Centuries were displayed along with handicraft and Nature Notebooks at the children's gatherings. And on at least one occasion, a school-wide Book of Centuries was "of great interest" as students would draw something from their current term's work and initial it as a keepsake. It would be lovely to hear such stories circulating again—people finding creative, relational ways to use the Book of Centuries, although perhaps today we might blog about it or share images on-line.

Teas and evenings of sharing are charming, but there is hidden value in the Book of Centuries beyond the community and shared experience. Talking to my son who studied history and politics for his undergraduate degree, the Book of Centuries came up in reference to his most recent interest, historiography. He explained that he was studying the history of studying history! The serious student of history must consider the different theories of how to best record or uncover what actually happened. It occurred to us that Mason not only lets her students read firsthand accounts and historical excerpts instead of compilations and textbooks, and not only do her students read history from several perspectives, for example, reading the history of France or that of the colonies concurrent to that being read of England, she actually adopts a method with the Book of Centuries that makes clear to the students every day in this subtle way that historians all have their own vantage point and perspective. By using the Book of Centuries, seeing that someone else considered the sinking of the Titanic the most important event in 1912, say, and not the introduction of the assembly line with Ford's model T, the student is well on his way, even at a young age, to a critical and academic reading of history which even some graduate students struggle to achieve. The classroom conversations that ensue: "why you chose that event as the most important, and I chose this," all through the faithful use of this one notebook, not only convey the notion of slant, they invite the Great Conversation about history and are the real work of the historian respectfully and remarkably entrusted as the real work of children.

Calendar of Events

There is one last picture in our gallery of forms, "Read the daily news and keep a calendar of events" is written on several of the programs for form IV and up.[181] The actual format of the calendar is not specified but clearly Mason wants some sort of diary of current events gathered from the child's world. As simple as a word or sentence jotted on a wall calendar creating a variation of the History Chart, (a likely platform for noticing that the History Chart is the Calendar of Events of yesterday), or as involved as a dated copybook containing the prose and poetic narrations of daily news, and even dictations —"calendar" is again being used in its more universal sense, as simply an ordering of dates. The style of the "keeping" is likely less important than the first half of the phrase, the reading of "the daily news." In much the same way as the Book of Centuries invites a critical approach to history, the Calendar of Events implicitly asks for all the students' conversations and learning to have the touch point of here and now. It is interesting that the directive is typically listed in the programs under English History and not Citizenship. Whatever form the Calendar took, it was likely secondary to the students being aware of their times and learning to discern and discuss the politics of their own nation and others in light of all the other reading they were doing––the Great Ideas in history, theology, literature, poetry and science.

The fact that there are only a few references and slight instructions for its structuring does not make this notebook inconsequential. On the contrary, we take it up last here, but certainly not least. Consider what the regular marking of national and world issues from middle school on along with a wide reading in all the liberal arts would give a student by the end of his school career. Mason concurs with apologist C.S. Lewis' championing of "old books" in this:

If you join at eleven o'clock a conversation which began at eight you will often not see the real bearing of what is said…The only safety is to have a standard of plain, central Christianity ("mere Christianity" as Baxter called it) which puts the controversies of the moment in their proper perspective. Such a standard can be acquired only from the old books. It is a good rule, after reading a new book, never to allow yourself another new one till you have read an old one in between. If that is too much for you, you should at least read one old one to every three new ones.[182]

But, next to reading pleasure, Mason is also after an enlivening of the "Classics" that were being read by schoolchildren in her day with the worthiest English literature and, characteristically, relationship. There was a point to reading the "books the world cannot do without."[183] To use Lewis' metaphor again, the students couldn't be expected to just join the conversation at eight either, armed with only bewildered Greek and Latin wanderings in Plato and Virgil. Thus, the Calendar of Events may be the principal invitation to the Great Conversation.[184] The realization dawns on the student slowly: "these are the Perennial Questions. I am reading the same ideas in the 18th Century as we were reading with the ancients and as are surfacing in issues today," without the teacher having to say such a word.

Lewis goes on in the introduction to a translation of Athanasius cited above to give what could be Mason's overarching rationale, not only for the Calendar of Events, but for education *in toto*; by reading in such a broad and connected way, we begin to perceive Glory.

That unity any of us can find by going out of his own age. It is not enough, but it is more than you had thought till then. Once you are well soaked in it (the wide reading), if you then venture to speak, you will have an amusing experience. You will be thought a Papist when you are actually reproducing Bunyan, a Pantheist when you are quoting Aquinas, and so forth. For you have now got on to the great level viaduct which crosses the ages and which looks so high from the valleys, so low from the mountains, so narrow compared with the swamps, and so broad compared with the sheep-tracks.

In just such a way, Mason would have the children outgrow the tight skin of the parochial or handed-down worldview, the dogmatic, or even nationalistic stance, and with their own keen minds (and lives) apply moral wisdom in their own day. "The tradition of the elders has been tried and found wanting."[185] In the same way that Mason returns the student again and again to Plutarch, the ancients, and the Old and New Testaments as they tackle the reading of each age, the Calendar of Events subtly invites the comparison and deep thought of Lewis' "viaduct," or what Mason calls the "intellectual commerce of ideas." Touch point is too mild a word; this is more like a revolutionary maneuver.

3

The Grand Invitation

"I enjoy the freedom of the blank page."

– Irene Welsh

"…how often the turning down this street or that, the accepting or rejecting of an invitation, may deflect the whole current of our lives into some other channel."

– Arthur Conan Doyle Sr.

In the previous chapter, we entertained a brief catalog of the sorts of notebooks specifically mentioned in Mason's volumes. We saw that with some of the practices we have a very clear picture; some of the books are perennial like the Nature Notebook, Book of Centuries, and Commonplace, and have very specific requirements; others come and go as the need arises and are more fluid and less defined. Though we have covered a lot of ground there are still many questions. We are left somewhat adrift: "Which book should we use and when?" "Who will tell us what to do?" "When does one practice stop and another begin?" In many cases, it appears we just don't know; in some we can surmise based on small textual clues. As frustrating as this can be, this aerial view of Mason's forms of vitality is a vantage point for seeing certain themes emerging that can inform our paper undertakings and ultimately satisfy most of our questions. Listed in the chart below (fig. 13) are descriptors Mason uses in her volumes and in *The Parents' Review* about these notebooks that when taken in a single view are very striking.

Notebook	Descriptors
Nature Notebook	companion, life record, very catholic, kept by the child, makes Science intimate, his initiative, his own management, not corrected, source of pride & joy, illustrated freely, source of delight.
Calendar of Firsts	looking for their favorites, new observations, Friends At Home, daily zest, interest, object.
Scrapbooks/collections	happy occupation, useful training.
Copybooks	beautiful, very pleasing script, passages of their choice.
Commonplace	passages with literary force or beauty, particular appeal to student, to cultivate taste, for striking thoughts of one's author, one's own impressions, short reviews, kept through life, exceedingly interesting, intellectual history of student.
Music Copybook	to produce the sign for a passage studied or sung.
"Enquire Within"	personal experience, how-to's, as she has done it or watched it done, invaluable, little special wrinkles.
My Word Book	his own capital, a place for friends.
Poetry Notebook	child chooses favorite verses, sense of possession & delight, to give them pleasure.
Student Yearbook/Motto Book	student culls from the best, delightful & stimulating, incentive to a good day, very own choice & selection, no outside mentor or direct teaching, endless subjects.
Fortitude Book (and others)	to fit our occasions, student chooses for himself.
Timelines and History Charts	child enters names as he comes on them, simple, graphic panorama, child sees time order.
Book of Centuries	life-long, a great joy to the owner, learning with their own connections, careful observation, personal, works of art, a great interest, a keen delight.

Fig. 13. Notebook Descriptors *(design Laurie Bestvater)*

While not exhaustive, typically when this chart is presented in a workshop, participants have an "aha" moment wherein they begin to see what Mason meant when she wrote, "Our conduct is the outcome of our principles."[186] I propose that the answers to some of our questions about Mason's use of forms of vitality begin with a deep appreciation for the principles undergirding them, her consistent rationale

Invariably, what is drawn from these few phrases is that the notebooks Mason favors are all highly personal, as all learning is highly personal. They are a unique framework for the child's own learning. Some are more formalized than others, but none are arbitrary or "busy work." The various paper activities proceed from Mason's philosophy that children are persons; the notebooks are tools for supporting the learning process of persons rather than products in and of themselves. Although some do eventually become keepsakes and the children should have guidelines and habitually do the best work they are able to do, our goal is not beautiful notebooks. The emphasis is not on the product but the formative process.

Carefully designed and selected over time to support her pedagogy by allowing for and encouraging reflection and relationship, Mason's notebooks are aptly named "forms of vitality." Taken as a whole, the notebooks emerge as the frame, the actual skeleton for the organic growth in the child we call learning. The Calendar of Firsts invites the child to make "friends" with the natural environment; the Poetry Notebook creates a personal attachment, line by line, to many great poems (and hence thoughts), a Fortitude Journal, or such like, feeds his inner life and character, as he has appetite with the tidbits he chooses for himself. The Enquire Within supports a life with things, acknowledges what philosopher and motorcycle guru Matthew Crawford calls "the cognitive richness of manual work" and the "ways of materials."[187] The practice of using these books is begun and buttressed by the atmosphere, discipline, and life of the school and teacher, but their content is clearly driven by the child and comprises a highly personalized journey and retelling.

Does that mean we must copy exactly what Mason has done? If so, we are in trouble since there are such holes in our knowledge, but perhaps we have enough in her examples and embedded principles to get started. It is easy enough to glean what she was after for what I call the three pillars: The Nature Notebook, The Book of Centuries, and the Commonplace, books she thinks should travel with us all our lives. With these we have enough to replicate her ways very closely; with some of the others it seems we are free, keeping within certain principles, to extract the essence and be more creative and flexible. For example, my students once kept a dollar store address book for an alphabetical listing of collective nouns," Kindle of Kittens" under "K," "Pod of Whales," "Bundle of Sticks," etc. This was a delight-driven activity in which the adaptation of an address book was merely a form for the vitality and the joy of collecting words. This is what I am suggesting as fluidity—the process being enhanced by an appropriate notebook. This particular notebook lasted only a short time, until the interest was satisfied. It would not be something I would assign to every student or classroom, rather an example of how the lesson and form can be adapted and kept living once we are clear about the "why" of our methods.

The main principle, the hard one to keep in view in our end-gaining society, is that Charlotte Mason's various paper activities are essentially instruments as opposed to artifacts; for process, more than product.[188] While this is by no means a disregard for the appropriate rigor, quality, or quantity of student work, the notebooks are singular means of beginning and solidifying relationships and individualized support for the student— his notebooks entries *are* the self-activity Mason is looking for in all the fullness that term implies. To see them as simply containers for the child's narrations is to overlook much of their real value. Mason's notebooks *invite* the noticing and attending—and are, in that sense, vital, organic and teeming with personality.

Therefore, where we do not have precise information on a notebook, we know we cannot err by allowing for process and structuring for "self-activity."[189] Mason bids her teachers to ensure the student engages in "the act of knowing." Narrating in its broadest sense, whether singing, dancing, drawing or retelling, is our masthead in all of the notebook practice. As we learn the philosophy and use of keeping what Reggio-Emilia educator, Ann Lewin-Benham, calls "open-ended" paper companions, we become more and more proficient in supporting our students in making their own connections and putting their stamp of personality on the material.[190] We no longer roam from desk to desk in our classrooms, instructing and prodding and adjusting our student's creations to fit our own firm mental picture. With the use of her notebooks, we come to see that Mason's equation is always: the written word or true-life thing + imagination = personal re-creation. We learn not to get in between, in the way of, the real life, primary source, or great author and the child's response.

Moreover, these various notebooks are means by which *we teachers* unwittingly learn the humility and art of respecting the child, of paying attention to each individual's learning process. We know through the archives that Mason's student teachers kept at least the Three Pillars while they were at the House of Education, i.e. a Nature Notebook, Book of

Centuries, and Commonplace. Teachers learning Mason's methods today could not do better than to keep these notebooks for themselves; the notebooks constrain us to transformation over information. We learn to ask different questions: "What are you thinking?" "Are you satisfied with your work?" "Is there anything you'd like to add?" "You seem to have a problem; do you want to talk about it?" "Do you want some help?" and sometimes even, "I need to ask you for more."[191]

Symbolized in the notebook workshops I give by my distribution of a blank sheet of paper, we are reminded that the forms of vitality require that no one stipulates, no one controls, no one demands a single, uniform outcome. Does this represent a complete unschooling, anything goes, Summerhill approach where the child is free to write or mark the page in any way he chooses? [192] No, clearly no; teachers may still, indeed must, specify—a written history narration or a particular map copied, or a poem composed in ballad form, is a productive and essential limit but the sifting and presentation of the content and noticing are all the child's.

It is an unusual method, a shift in paradigm even, but consistent use of these various forms of vitality actually serves to engender relationships and the habits of noticing so integral to the inner life and all true learning.[193] The blank page and the open-ended question stop us, may even make us slightly uncomfortable; what have we with which to fill the notebook? As such, we have just the right level of relaxed alertness required for learning that teachers usually have to work so hard to achieve.[194] Ultimately, the blank page makes us examine our thoughts for metacognition, and intrinsically, it insists upon space and time for learning.

Artist Georgia O'Keeffe, well-known American painter of the gigantic, exquisitely detailed flowers, knowingly remarked about her ability, "in a way, nobody sees a flower, really, it is so small. We haven't time—and to see takes time, like to have a friend takes time."[195] With her science of relations, and as a gracious hostess, Mason invites with time and means, her students to see, to make friends.[196]

And is that not why our notebooks become dear to us? *I come back to my original question: Why do I have so many notebooks?* Mason helps me answer: personalizing my learning and capturing some of it in turn inspires me to more relationships and more learning. Because they are never done, these notebooks help me to notice, to become ever more awake to the world around me, and to live in it more fully. Is this not the Mason paradigm shift on paper?[197] Is not this life with notebooks an effort to attend, to really see?

Could the science of relations also be called the fine art of noticing, the life of mindfulness? "Knowing glory when we see it?" There is a reason Mason is always on about attention. As Brazilian author Paulo Coelho writes, "You can become blind by seeing each day as a similar one. Each day is a different one; each day brings a miracle of its own. It's just a matter of paying attention to this miracle."[198] Mason invites us to nurture this sacramental approach to life through her notebooks. It is as if she says, "Come, join me, and look." In becoming Keepers we are compelled to pay close attention to the relationships and details all around us and "… to a child who perceives these things miracles will not be matters of supreme moment because *all life will be for him matter for wonder and adoration*"[199] (emphasis mine.)

Again, we find Mason relying on a profound intuition and common sense that is resonating with some of today's educators. She arrives with a determination to hold onto that which educational researcher Brenda Rees notices our short answer and fill-in-the-blank world has almost lost track of, "that student learning is greatly enhanced when students are empowered to make decisions related to how they connect new content to what they already know, organize their thoughts, and communicate their understanding of newly acquired concepts."[200]

Our paper friends, by their very natures, have important things to whisper to us. The Book of Centuries, then, is more than a way to record historical facts, even more than getting a sense of the flow of history or the forming of a relationship with the artifacts and grandeur of humankind's unfolding; it also positions us to hear the critical approach to history and invites us to take our own place, a place no other can fill, in the unfolding drama. A Keeper is a learner awake. For instance, as Dr. Lynee Gaillet observes, the Commonplace "makes concrete the assumption that readers are potential writers."[201] It attunes us not only to the inner life but to the Great Conversation.

> A commonplace book is also an aid to self-education and memory. Keeping one forces you to become an active reader, to read with one eye towards the main points of an argument, the beautiful quote, the insight that gives you pause. You become aware of more than just the words on the page; you become aware of the author's arguments, his writing style, and what **you** think about what the author is saying. It creates a give-and-take between writer and

reader. Furthermore, the act of writing down quotations and arguments fixes them more firmly in the memory, making it more likely that you'll remember them at appropriate times. Periodically re-reading your commonplace book will further strengthen your recall even more.[202]

The ongoing use of Word Books, Copybooks, Poetry Notebooks, and Commonplaces speaks an unconscious but powerful message about the Great Conversation: "it is worth having, and I too have a voice." The deep reading of the work of others that feeds this life and is laid before us in these practices is not just about gathering collective nouns, stylistic options, or the ability to match prose to an audience or employ problem-solving strategies, though, as Gaillet points out, it does all those things very well. But these forms of vitality woo us, whisper a welcome into all that is best in a full human life.[203]

And this is not just a paper and words life; Mason posits a profoundly reunited education by "books and things."[204] The Nature Notebook not only leads to "significant gains in student achievement" and elevates the scientific discourse of the class, it chants the expectation of glory and anticipates the daily mystery that will open before us through the physical realm.[205] The Enquire Within insists on "the satisfactions of manifesting oneself concretely in the world through the manual competencies (that) have been known to make a man quiet and easy" that Crawford and others so long for.[206] The blank page is our invitation to the banquet—and all of its courses.

Conversely, the use of textbooks and preprinted pages sends "the message that the world is best interacted with by completing disposable worksheets that involve filling in the blank, circling true or false, choosing a, b, c, or d, or drawing an arrow from something in column a to something in column b."[207] Armstrong goes so far as to say the glossy pages of commercially produced curriculum are a "major hazard."[208]

Even in the classroom, Mason asserts what Canadian philosopher Marshall McLuhan would notice a century later, that the "medium is the message."[209] If a person can only be built up from within, what else but the freedom of blank page transmits that confidence? Is it too much to say a child's growth and transformation demand these open-ended postures, that Mason's forms of vitality are an imperative to true education and the Grand Invitation?

4

"Setting Up Self-Activity"

"I am not a teacher but an awakener. "

– Robert Frost

"To arouse wonder and admiration must be one of the teacher's principal aims."

– Essex Cholmondley

It seems ridiculous to point out that chapter four follows chapter three and that three follows two, but there it is: I need to draw attention to the fact that I have left most of the practical questions about Mason's notebooks for next to last. I do so because although it is a commonplace that teaching is an art, it has been my experience that Mason's "fine art of standing aside" is not so easily grasped. It takes a teacher deeply immersed in Mason's writings and practice, especially in what Neil Postman calls our culture of "scientism,"[210] to *"safeguard the initiative of the child,"* intuit the right level of support and encouragement for each individual child's best discovery and growth.[211] Often the prevailing worldview creates an anxiety to "get on with it," and drives the beginner to want the practice before the theory or even instead of the theory. I distinctly remember hearing about narration for the first time and thinking to myself, "what an utter waste of time. I have material to get through!" I had no understanding. I was simply looking at a practice without seeing the underpinnings and it looked unreasonable, untenable even. We can, in our admirable concern to "do a good job," easily miss what Mason is saying, so wonderfully echoed by poet Robert Frost above: we are awakeners. If our besetting question is, "how do I do this?" we may need to pause a while over that fine "art of standing aside." We may need to review Mason's unhurried rhythms to adjust our pace before considering the practical out-workings I have attempted to gather from her writings and lay out in this chapter.

If teachers are undertaking the almost invisible task of nurturing these comfortable friendships with notebooks, they are doing as Mason advised in setting up the self-activity.[212] They are not selecting the exact content for the notebooks, but they are making themselves familiar with the parameters and genius of each venue, looking over the day's work to see where certain kinds of narrations suggest themselves, balancing the written, drawn, sung, painted, acted, etc. and generally curating the feast so that the notebooks become (over time) a natural means of response. The atmosphere of responding and habits listed below will be general to all the notebooks and, once assimilated, will allow these paper postures to give great pleasure to their owners. Mason teachers spend much of their thought and effort on the nuances of the forms, the needs of each learner, and on cultivating a classroom atmosphere that will foster "self-activity."

That atmosphere begins with the respect shown the child—the expectation that he can respond and can do good work. "Slipshod work should not be allowed; therefore, the children's work should be kept well within their compass. No work should be given to a child that he cannot execute *perfectly,* and then perfect execution should be expected of him as a matter of course."[213]

Yet we hold that expectation with good humor, in tension with the fact that the children's abilities will continue to improve. "The first buttercup in a child's nature notebook is shockingly crude, the sort of thing to scandalise a teacher of brush-drawing, but by and by another buttercup will appear with the delicate poise, uplift, and radiance of the growing flower."[214] We look for ways to scaffold and are patient. We let the children do their own rightful and meaningful work. This is a deeply countercultural approach in many cases, as the teacher below describes.

> When I taught kindergarten, I was appalled at how many times teachers would have their assistants cut out construction paper flowers or frogs or whatever else, and then they would have the children use sparkles or crayons or googly eyes to decorate them and call it art so it could be displayed in a row in the hallway for parent night. That is an extreme

example, but one of the requirements for accreditation at the _____School was to have samples of student work displayed in the room. Many times special projects were created just for this purpose. The same "for what purpose?" sentiment goes for science fair projects and conservation poster contests. But I have found also that many parents want to see cute little products and worksheets come home in the weekly folders because that is the only way they think they can know their child has been doing something in school. Some have trouble seeing the value of oral activities or notes/drawings that reflect process. (Teachers do generally see the value in these things, but they continue to plan "activities" so they can have something to display in the classroom or send home on Monday afternoon.) [215]

Parents also need time to assimilate that "notebook" is actually a misnomer. We are not note-taking at all; by notebooks we simply refer to Mason's various paper activities. They may need help to see that their child's notebooks are not primarily products or even mainly for the display of the student's learning. The teacher may describe the various purposes at work in practical examples during parent/teacher interactions. A parent can be shown that a rough sketch of a painting from memory is a narration and though not particularly attractive in itself, indicative of a great mental effort, whereas a copy of the whole painting might be a product for the sake of the product, making it a different activity altogether.

> Children from six to nine describe the picture, giving all the details and showing by a few lines where is such a tree or such a house; judging if they can the time of day; discovering the story if there be one. The older children add to this some study of the lines of composition, light and shade, the particular style of the master, and reproduce from memory certain details. *The object of these lessons is that the pupils should learn how to appreciate rather than how to produce.*[216] (emphasis mine)

Parents can come to see in concrete ways how the rationale of Mason's student-produced books, excepting copy work, [217] of course, is not so much to directly reproduce knowledge but to allow personality to work on what has been taken in.[218]

Teachers' Notebooks

The teacher in a Mason learning community is a co-learner, and it is very helpful for a teacher to model to his students (and parents) that his own learning also includes some comfortable notebook friends. As educators like Ann Lewin-Benham are discovering in Vygotsky, Mason hits the nail on the head.

> Followers of Vygotsky, many of whom are leading psychologists, believe that materials have most influence on learning when they are used together with another human. More than just together with, children learn best when an adult interacts in the process of using materials and when learning takes place as a social or collaborative process. Current research in neuroscience confirms many of Vygotsky's theories.[219]

With a room full of young children, working in her notebook may not be possible for the busy teacher, but the wise head of school will look for ways to ensure that the life, atmosphere, and discipline being shared has space and time for this important part of the teachers' practice. Mason's students at the House of Education and in the Mother's Course kept notebooks and apart from being good for the students, it seems a very good way to support the paradigm shift for the teacher, not to mention a great personal satisfaction.[220] As noted earlier, the Three Pillars, the Commonplace, the Nature Notebook, and The Book of Centuries, would seem the natural beginning place for teachers.

Materials

"…boxes of cheap colours are to be avoided. Children are worthy of the best."[221]

It only stands to reason that Mason's respect for the student and her insistence on the use of real things would necessitate simple, good quality materials. While Mason might not go to the extent of Waldorf educators and stipulate the use of only natural materials, the cheap and tawdry have no place in her schema. Her biographer notes "inside the book (i.e. the Nature Notebook) is nothing more than good drawing paper (for painting without pencil lines) and there is the understanding that children should have whatever materials we would want to use ourselves.[222] Mason talks about the delight in making and having "power over material" which suggests building student familiarity with a variety of resources.[223] In *Home Education*, we read, "An exercise book with stiff covers serves for a nature diary, but care is necessary in choosing paper that answers both for writing and brush drawing."[224] Clearly, if the students are going to enjoy their notebooks, they must be of good quality and attractive. Since some of these books will travel with the child over many subjects and several years, durability is also a prime consideration. Under certain circumstances, a family or a class may share a notebook, such as a Family Diary, Calendar of Firsts, or Timeline, but given Mason's emphasis on self-activity, each student should ideally have his own notebooks and supplies, just as she insists he is to have his own school books.[225]

Coloring Books, Clipart, Worksheets and Visual Aids

Mason is adamant that children strengthen their imaginations; and to that end coloring books, clip art, and worksheets are largely put aside. Her words of 1925 might have been written today:

> Great confidence is placed in diagrammatic and pictorial representation, and it is true that children enjoy diagrams and understand them as they enjoy and understand puzzles; but there is apt to be in their minds a great gulf between the diagram and the fact it illustrates. We trust much to pictures, lantern slides, cinematograph displays [movies]; but without labour there is no profit, and probably the pictures which remain with us are those which we have first conceived through the medium of words; pictures may help us to correct our notions, but the imagination does not work upon a visual presentation; we lay the phrases of a description on our palette and make our own pictures; (works of art belong to another category).[226]

As a rule of thumb, it is after the words (or experiences) are digested as thoroughly as possible and the best picture we can come up with formed in our minds, that we look at photographs, diagrams, models, movies and the like to clarify anything still unclear. And that only occasionally; real life is always preferable to the image. In this way, we instruct the imagination so that wherever our mind picture does not line up with reality we may learn to better understand the next verbal description we come across.[227] With things like worksheets, coloring books, and clip art, somebody else has already done much of the selecting and connecting, and that limits rather than enhances self-activity.

Role of Technology

Still, in a digital world, the question must arise: why preserve the paper and pencil approach of a notebook? We have media at our disposal that Mason would have found astounding. Today, a Commonplace may be kept conveniently as a blog, include photographs and video with endless cut and paste options like Tumblr or Pinterest. It is possible to compose a nature notebook of sorts out of one's personal photos in a digital format rather than with dry brush paintings. A Current Events Journal could be compiled as a doc file. Are physical notebooks passé?

Most assuredly, this question takes its place in the Great Conversation of our day: when does technology make us less and not more human? What are its limits? Like most such questions, there are no simple answers. The full extent of the Internet's effect on the brain and human development and on culture is only starting to be considered. Mason was a keen follower of the science of her day, especially the brain research, so we can assume she would welcome the conversation and probably even some of technology's advances.[228] And yet, likely she would have recognized, as philosopher and cultural critic Neil Postman argues in *Amusing Ourselves to Death*, the implicit dangers of an over-dependence on technology. People are beginning to notice that the digital life is changing how we read and attend; it affects our epistemology, our ways of knowing.[229] Pioneer that she was, even in the early 1900's, Mason thinks the use of "devices" must be carefully weighed.

> The simplicity and power in the teacher of illustrating by
> inkpot and ruler or any object at hand, or by a few lines on
> the blackboard, appears to me to be of more use than the

most elaborate equipment of models and diagrams; these things stale on the sense and produce a torpor of thought the moment they are presented.[230]

We must follow the discussion, to be sure. Doubtless, there are many ways we may be helped by the latest technology in our efforts to educate like Mason—using voice recognition software to record and transcribe for pre-writing narrators, taking photos of specimen to paint from rather than capturing and possibly harming insects or missing the intricacy of a bird's wing in a quick sighting, sharing line drawings well suited to the Book of Centuries through the Internet with students around the world, are only a few. These are some uses that do not seem to contravene the principles of the human education she proposes but rather enhance relationship in the ways she was after. For instance, I can Google a folk song and instantly have several YouTube renditions from which to choose. My older students have even made more of a connection to their music studies by doing just that, creating their own CD or smartphone playlist of favored artists performing each piece on the syllabus. Yet ultimately, nothing can replace the formative weight of finally singing that folksong as many times as necessary to have it by heart. In following Mason's design for education, we face the prospect of innovation with a healthy reserve, sometimes in the camp of Wendell Berry, American artist Makoto Fujimura, and others, who decline to lose the attention, observation, meditation, and art of the handwritten or drawn. As Berry sagely notes, "my standards are not speed, ease, and quantity. I have already left behind too much evidence that, writing with a pencil, I have written too fast, too easily, and too much. I would like to be a better writer, and for that I need help from other humans, not a machine."[231]

As teachers and students, we will continue to wrestle with what Communications professor Quentin Schultz calls, this "…most important question…whether our cyber-practices are making us better persons and our society more civil and democratic."[232] Hopefully, we will land more often than not in a place that preserves a pace and structure for mindfulness and human flourishing as we explore all of the wonders of the 21st century.

Guidelines for Student Work

"Self-activity" should not imply, however, a lack of structure. Each notebook has its impetus within the method, and habit is no less a feature of

The Living Page

this aspect of a Mason education. Students will not naturally know how to keep a Commonplace or a Book of Centuries. They must be prepared by the teacher and maintain certain habits with their notebooks if these are to give pleasure and do as they are meant to do. I cannot forget the novice who handed the class the beautiful hardcover Nature Notebooks with creamy white watercolor stock *before* instructing them about the use of watercolors or even where to put their names. The class was not in the habit of cherishing a notebook but accustomed to worksheets and other consumable items, and it never occurred to them that they should not spatter their opening pages with various colors from their paint boxes or etch their names and even a skull and crossbones on one, into the cover with a sharp pencil! As with any friendship, introductions must be made, etiquette attended to, if the relationship is to be gratifying. Below are some general suggestions for keeping notebooks culled from experience, followed by more specific guidelines for the "Three Pillars" with the hopes that they may inform cases where there are choices to be made and a form is adaptable to a teacher's or student's preference. These are not meant to be a Mason legalism, rather to release the students and teachers from the burden of a sad experience or a less than satisfactory result. Again, the distinction is made: notebook habits, at least in the beginning, are teacher specified but dealing with the content is less so.[233]

General Habits for Keeping Notebooks

Neatness, order, beauty, and perfect execution are highly esteemed in Mason's pedagogy, so the habit of expecting and getting only the student's best work should be cultivated. The wise teacher will give various supports so that a child is not frustrated by an expectation beyond his ability; he is assigned only that which he is fully able to do. For example, a child has learned his letters at a chalkboard or white board with the chance of a quick erasure until all is right before being asked to copy four careful renderings into his copybook. If the date is wanted, as most times it will be, the teacher will talk on several occasions about the days of the week and demonstrate the convention of writing dates, which can be different amongst cultures, on the chalkboard and eventually notice where on the page the date always lives. The children will begin with pencil until they can manage well with ink. They may be given light pencil lines if they feel their script is apt to travel uphill, and then instructed on the uses of a straight edge. Children must be comfortable with all the media they encounter before they attempt a notebook application. Watching a seventh grader who had obviously never held a paintbrush struggle with a dry brush painting in his new nature notebook showed his teacher that all that paint mixing and big brush work at the easel in the early years has its place, is actually a way of showing respect to a child, as it would eventually enable him to be at home with his old friend the paintbrush.[234] Let them find out that leads in colored pencils are no good if dropped. It seems only experience tells that sharpening incessantly is fun but leads to smudge marks on one's page or clothes; afterwards provide a means for sharpened pencils that respects everyone and his work.

Before every lesson, until the notebook protocol becomes automatic, the teacher respects her students by recalling how to proceed *before* the notebooks are opened or even retrieved from the shelf, much as a lab teacher might give guidelines for the use of lab equipment or the format for the writing up of experiments. The teacher can give a little of the rationale for the book or introduce its use in an interesting way, perhaps giving the history of commonplaces or looking at some historical models as the child moves from Copybook to Commonplace. It may be helpful to show student work from other schools or classes so that the child gets an idea of what is possible. In these simple and unassuming ways, the teacher can introduce and create the means for the budding friendship or conversely create a distaste or aversion with rigid remarks and disapproval.

Teachers of young children may not be able to accompany them in painting as their hands are needed to help but middle-schoolers often strengthen their relationship with the practice through a teacher who obviously loves keeping her own Nature Notebook or Book of Centuries and is disciplined about its use. In school settings, let the children in first form know they are embarking on a school-wide, cherished tradition in keeping a Calendar of Firsts or that their Nature Notebook will be with them, hopefully all their lives. Develop little traditions and celebrations like a Book of Centuries tea (or picnic?) that allow the forms of vitality to contribute to the atmosphere as the atmosphere becomes part of the forms of vitality—the science of relations. Practice giving enough time for an activity; frustration ensues when beginning a dry brush drawing that one cannot finish because the bus is here or we have to go to music lesson. If a thing is going to take more than one sitting, as a Book of Centuries drawing might, or map work, explain that ahead of time and help the students come to a self-generated proposal of how the work might be split up.

Guidelines for the Three Pillars

Book of Centuries

This notebook is begun at about age ten (about the second year of Form II) when handwriting has become more secure. In the beginning, the teacher may want to encourage finding the proper space on the chart with a finger, noting that the numbers reverse from BCE and CE, before a pen is ever taken up. The student may even practice writing the word on a piece of scrap paper for size and spelling before neatly entering it on the correct page and line. The Book of Centuries I have published modeled after Bernau's has wee dots at the top of each chart which can be used to draw a light pencil line to indicate the column for more support for the beginner, but I would not leave the lines in as the page is much more effective without them and Bernau did not use them. Soon there will be five elegant "lists" running down the page in the child's own hand.

Another fear is making a sketching mistake, and Bernau anticipates it by making mention of students sketching lightly in pencil before using ink. (Just don't try to erase the pencil before the ink is completely dry!) There is nothing wrong with doing a practice sketch on scrap paper. Pilot makes an extra fine black pen called the "Razor" which is very satisfactory for this type of drawing and there are others that do not bleed or blot the page. Encourage the student to hold the pen as if they were sketching and not to press too hard. The student should also be encouraged not to select artifacts to draw that are too difficult so they do not become frustrated but are proud of their work. Bernau allows that more complex drawings may be saved for later with the reassurance that skill will grow.[235] It might be tempting to cut out a picture or a photocopy in such cases, but Bernau says generally pictures are not glued in as that could also contribute to a book appearing messy and becoming "too bulky."[236] The students benefit most by drawing artifacts with the slow noticing of one's subject which that requires. The drawings rarely, if ever, include color, as the effect of the pen and ink gives a unity that hides slight imperfections. Students may be encouraged to know that perfection is not expected but just their neatest effort.[237] Bernau comfortingly emphasizes that the books are to be neat and accurate but one need not be an artist to make one.

The Commonplace

Any durable hardcover with good paper can serve for the Commonplace and there is no end to the beautiful blank notebooks available today. Students may like to choose their own with a little guidance, or schools may have special books printed with their logo or motto. Most prefer lined as opposed to blank pages, and a good sewn binding will allow the book to survive for many years. Some thought should be given to how flat the book lies open for the younger writer, but spiral bound books, while flexible, are generally less satisfactory in the long run and often contain a lesser quality paper. If the paper is thin, suggest the students write on only one side of the page for a more attractive book. Teachers may even want to include lessons in bookbinding and allow students to make their own Commonplaces; there are several methods that could be studied as handiwork.

Mason does not specify an age for beginning the Commonplace. Likely somewhere around middle school the child transitions to a freer use of copy work that would suggest its use. The P.N.E.U. programs definitely show it being relied on in high school and it is meant to be a lifelong companion. Andrew Gudgel notes that the contents of a commonplace are traditionally quite varied, and we have no reason to think Mason wants anything other—like the Nature Notebook, the Commonplace is likely "very catholic" and personal.[238] She does specify that it contain quotes that have inspired the reader, passages of the "best kind" of writing that cultivate taste, and the words that make a spiritual impact. Though she mentions the odd character sketch from a novel, the Commonplace is not for collecting literature narrations, journaling, or compositions by the student. This is a treasury of ideas and inspiration. Beyond that, we have little practical information. Sometimes Mason refers to the Commonplace as a Reading Diary and it has made sense to some students to include a list of books read (title, author and date), starting on the back page and working forwards. A similar list of books one wishes to read may also be kept. Some writers developed indexing systems for their commonplaces, most notably Erasmus and Locke, but nothing I have seen suggests that Mason had thoughts about this one way or another. Likely that can also be left to the writer's discretion. Students may appreciate looking at on-line and archived commonplaces from famous people like George Washington and others for inspiration, and it is a good idea for the teacher to spend some time introducing the practice and discussing the options. The teacher will also work to transition the child from being asked if there is anything he wants to include in his Commonplace to handing over responsibility for its use to the student.

The Nature Notebook

Likewise, time for the Nature Notebook will have to be presented by the teacher at first, at least weekly, preferably daily, as the student gradually becomes the self-learner who relies on this companionship unconsciously. Instruction about dry brush technique, positioning the specimen on the page, observing quietly and carefully before starting will be part of all early lessons with a goal of independence. It may seem practical for beginners to all work from the same specimen at first, but the teacher will want to move them to choosing their own items for painting very quickly after the protocol is secure since the literature indicates that it is the choosing and looking that Mason is after. Things like outlining the shape in a light yellow paint that may be colored over, adding the date in pencil, painting on only one side of the page, how to "dry" the brush on the edge of the glass or on a bit of paper towel need to be reinforced regularly in the early days while still allowing the children personal management of their books. Care of the paint box and brush will be demonstrated, and how one may mix the paint in the lid. Some guidance is given as to the kind of things that can be written to accompany the painting: how to find the Latin name or family in a guidebook, where the specimen was found and under which conditions, interesting observations or accompanying folklore or verse may be added (even in another class period if time is short). The teacher will help students create life lists and calendars of sightings in the back of the book, students and teachers agreeing on a format that is simple and useful.[239]

When to Use a Notebook?

By now it will be apparent that there are few hard and fast rules about using most of Mason's notebooks. We survey the possibilities, watch for the student's spark of connection, and use our discretion and creativity to suggest a "form." Some notebooks are used for just a short while as we master a skill, like the Word Book, and others we keep all our lives, like the Book of Centuries. Indeed, it is hard to think of a modern equivalent, a book that travels through all our classes and grades. As Bernau writes, "Children get accustomed to treating their 'Books of Centuries' as companions to all their reading."[240] Obviously, the Book of Centuries is a part of history lessons, but it also takes its place in Citizenship, Literature, Art, and even Science and Music. As Mrs. Brown writes in *The Parents' Review*, this can be surprising.

We have found the Century Books invaluable. In connection with our music they are a great help. Each musician as
he is studied in his turn (one each 12 week term) is entered
in the century book in his own century among his contemporaries, with the artists, scientists, writers, historical
characters and events of his own period. This gives us the
proper perspective which is necessary to the understanding
and enjoyment of his music. The children who have this
historical perspective do not, when listening to an air by
Purcell, expect the sort of music they would hear if they
were listening to Wagner. Thanks to the century books
they put the music against its proper background.[241]

So the Books of Centuries are very "catholic" like the Nature Notebooks
which may be used for Art, Science, Natural History and Geography,
Poetry, and even as a travel record. And like the Commonplace, the passages selected come from the student's reading in any and every subject; it
is the spark of connection (Life?) that motivates its use and which cannot
be confined to a single subject or class period. The Enquire Within deals
largely with real life things and the practical activities in a Mason education, but it could also find uses in several subject areas, recording how to
make compost or set up a hotbed in Science, including instructions for
mixing colors for dry brush painting or carding wool for Handicraft, or
even to record directions for using the subway to get to the Metropolitan
Museum of Art. Once the teachers (and then students) know the possibilities, the right notebook for a narration will present itself. Some things may
appear in different forms in several notebooks. For example, I may record
Dickens' death in my Book of Centuries, write a passage of dialogue from
his novel in my Fortitude Journal, and list *Tale of Two Cities* as a "Book
Read" in the back of my Commonplace. I may search for a bird he mentions in his writing and having seen it, paint it in my Nature Notebook
with a quote from the book. But this is not a unit study on Dickens because
as the student, I am waiting for my own spiritual response to the material
and choosing what is piquing my interest. At times, there is no spark of life,
no notebook entry suggests itself from a certain book or author, and that
is to be expected, too. The main thing is that the teacher and the student
come to know what is possible and the notebooks' protocols so that they
really are comfortable friends that accompany one's learning expeditions.

How to Start with Notebooks

Though Mason depends on certain of the notebooks and specifies their use to various degrees, when to add a notebook and how to organize student work must still be organic to the school, teacher, and student. Personality is involved. "Neatness is akin to order but is not quite the same thing: it implies not only 'a place for everything, and everything in its place,' but everything in a suitable place, so as to produce a good effect; in fact, taste comes into play."[242] We follow the spirit of the law and not the letter; maps, narrations, math tests—there is no perfect way to order it all, no Mason "system." We are after the "suitable," "tasteful" solution to "good effect" all the while keeping the particular notebook and principles of her pedagogy in mind.

Newcomers to Keeping will likely want to start simply with just one or two of the notebooks and will add each "friend" in a natural and easy way. It is utterly feasible to begin with just a Nature Notebook and one other notebook that receives both narrations and copy work if adding the others seems burdensome. Those and the Parent Yearbook (or Teacher Yearbook) can carry the beginner a long way. (All other paper can be simply collected for a student in a new file folder each term). Personhood, atmosphere, good habits and life must all be respected and maintained if these notebooks are to become friends rather than critics. In our eagerness for the beauty we see revealed in Mason's view of education, we can forget that many of these layers are built up over years, not weeks or months. In providing the chart below (fig.14) depicting the notebooks as they appear across the years, I reiterate that in some cases these are only my best surmises and that although I am convinced they represent the *kind* of work Mason was after, they were almost certainly *never* used all at once.

In some instances, there will be no guidance given by Mason for a certain classroom need, for example, "where do we do our math problems?" A spiral-bound notebook or a folder to collect loose pages may be an equally satisfactory answer. Art prints downloaded and easily printed on single sheets require a different solution than when they arrived in their own bound volumes from the printer as they did in Mason's day. One might want to keep a three ring binder for each student with plastic sleeves to receive each print of a term's painter and perhaps written or sketched narrations. With personal computers widely available, a teacher may accept narrations that have been typed from time to time and collate the best in a portfolio or an accordion file for the student. Other narrations may be done in a hardbound book that becomes the student's own History of the World. There are some options.

Likewise, an almost endless variety of boxes, baskets and bins can contain student work in an aesthetically pleasing way. A wire farm basket can hold a class set of nature notebooks, "bibs" with pockets for notebooks can be sewn for the backs of unattractive plastic chairs, and cloth bags made ready to tote supplies for nature walks. Dividers, file boxes, clip boards, baskets, bushel barrels can all be called into service. One school I know approached a pizza shop to get flat, unmarked cardboard boxes to house individualized student collections. We can be flexible and creative. Once the principles and options are understood, variations and adaptations are not only possible but desirable in the face of individual needs.

Evaluating Notebooks

"It is a good idea, then, to keep in touch, and I suppose that keeping in touch is what notebooks are all about. And we are all on our own when it comes to keeping those lines open to ourselves: your notebook will never help me, nor mine you."[243] Didion intuits as Mason did, that a person is built up from within. She is right in that no one can do our learning for us, but as a teacher, your notebook most certainly *will* help me. As researcher Brenda Rees observes:

> For students, notebooks are a place where they gather data, communicate their understanding, and reflect on what they learned. For teachers, student notebook entries are windows into student thinking, providing valuable information about what they know and don't know. Thus, a student notebook is an important instructional tool, which can be used to design targeted interventions.[244]

While experts will see all the intricacies of student assessment in Mason's model of education, some of the benefits of this method are readily apparent. In observing the child's connections to the material unfold with the notebook, the teacher quickly knows how to adjust the next day's lesson, provide a visual aid, have a weaker child narrate a shorter passage, or go more deeply into an unexpected area of interest. This is feedback at its most immediate and effective, largely eliminating the need for disembodied and tiresome tests and quizzes.

:: Notebooks become a record of work done. It is surprising how their simple existence can give a sense of the rich life of the schoolroom and the children's handling of the Great Ideas.

:: Notebooks allow the teacher to see quickly if the habits or protocols for organization are followed (these can be listed in the back page of the book or with a sticky note.) This offers opportunity for discussion with the student: "Which have you met, not met and why, what is the difficulty?" "Explain why we need the date or straight columns?"—i.e. neatness respects the other people who might join this conversation through the notebook.

:: While we do not focus on a number or letter grade, students appreciate the occasional respectful comment from a teacher, perhaps on a post-it note or piece of stationery tucked between the pages (so as not to take liberties with their books.) These are not evaluations necessarily but the teacher's own genuine thoughts on the Great Conversation represented in the student's book. For example:
"Oh, I had the same thought when I read this."
"Wow, I hadn't thought of that."
"This is interesting; did you know such and so also wrote…."
"Have you seen the play acted out?" etc.
We don't want students to depend on our approval but we do want to share the experience with them.[245]

:: Students naturally self-evaluate when sharing their notebooks with others, so partnering or showing work to parents will be a fruitful part of the atmosphere. Naturally, too many questions asked at once would be an affront, but the following are some approaches a partner, parent, or teacher may find appropriate for a particular learning moment:
"Which parts of this are you most satisfied with?"
"Is there something you are longing to add?"

"What do you think would make this better?"

"Did you learn anything about keeping this notebook that you want to incorporate next time?"

"Did you get any ideas from your partner?"

"Did you feel you did your best work?"

"Did you tell/draw all you remember?"

"Did you have enough time or do you need to find more time to work on this?"

:: Notebooks are constantly evaluated in the teacher's daily interactions with the students. Habits and inspiration are held out for their improvement as part of the culture of "kid-watching" and each child encouraged individually to stretch just a little above his level. Therefore, notebooks are evaluated in terms of the student's own progress and not a teacher's standard or peer ability.

Forms of Vitality across the Years

Nature

Nature Notebook

K*	**X** Paint, draw but do not print - dictate notes. May begin as family diary.
Form I	**X** Paint, draw describe mostly dictate. "Find and describe six wild fruits, 10 birds, five other animals per term & special studies.
Form II	**X** Paint, draw, describe. Experiments where possible.
Form III	**X** Paint, draw. Flower & bird lists. Daily notes. Experiments where possible. Special studies for the season.
Form IV	**X** Paint, draw. Flower & bird lists. Daily notes. Experiments where possible. Special studies for the season.
Forms V, VI	**X** Paint, draw. Flower & bird lists. Daily notes. "Choose special studies. Specimens should be used in all botanical work. Experiments must be made."
Life	**X**

Calendar of Firsts

K*	**X** may begin as a family diary.
Form I	**X**
Form II	**X**
Form III	**X**
Form IV	**X**
Forms V, VI	**X** may lead to ecological and community work.
Life	X inferred.

Scrapbooks & Collecting

K*	**X** informal collecting and display encouraged.
Form I	**X** "mount in scrapbook six wild flowers (per term?) with leaves, know their names & whether they grow in field, hedge, or marsh."
Form II	**X** Twenty plants or parts of plants mounted as specimens.
Form III	**X** Mounting not mentioned specifically, but specimens are used for study.
Form IV	**X** Mounting not mentioned specifically, but specimens are used for study.
Forms V, VI	**X** Mounting not mentioned specifically, but specimens are used for study.
Life	Teachers sometimes pressed plants in Nature Notebook.

Language

Word Book

K*	**X** Informal, child may be ready for this in third trimester.
Form I	**X** Beginning reader takes stock of "his possessions in the way of words."
Form II	Needed only remedially once reading is fluent in mother tongue.

Poetry Book

K*	
Form I	**X** transcribe slowly in beautiful work verses (not whole poems) which the child chooses from reading.
Form II	**X** Choose and transcribe in beautiful writing from poetry reading.
Form III	**X** Choose and transcribe in beautiful writing from poetry reading. Uncertain—the role of the poetry notebook seems to be taken over by the Commonplace (perhaps in Form III).
Form IV	Uncertain—the role of the poetry notebook seems to be taken over by the Commonplace (perhaps in Form III).
Forms V, VI	Uncertain—the role of the poetry notebook seems to be taken over by the Commonplace (perhaps in Form III).

Copybook/Commonplace

K*	Letter play.
Form I	**X Copybook** Transcribe letters, then short phrases, then building up to sentences from his reading.
Form II	**X Copybook** Transcribe longer passages of interest from his reading, carefully moving to script when ready.
Form III	**X Commonplace** may begin–exact age not specified. Teacher gradually eases student into habit and independent choice of all passages.
Form IV	**X Commonplace** Transcribe passages of literary force or beauty that appeal to student. To cultivate taste.
Forms V, VI	**X Commonplace** Transcribe passages of literary force or beauty that appeal to student. To cultivate taste.
Life	X

French Notebook (a Word Book for 2nd language)

K*	
Form I	**X** Teacher keeps.
Form II	**X** Teacher keeps until child is fluent and begins reading second language.
Form III	**X** Teacher keeps until child is fluent and begins reading second language, then uncertain, student could keep, gradually adding functions of the Poetry Book, Copybook, and Commonplace (Notebook for third language can begin and follow the same progression).
Form IV	X uncertain, student could keep, gradually adding functions of the Poetry Book, Copybook, and Commonplace (Notebook for third language can begin and follow the same progression).
Forms V, VI	X uncertain, student could keep, gradually adding functions of the Poetry Book, Copybook, and Commonplace functions (Notebook for additional languages can begin and follow the same progression).
Life	

Ourselves

Parent Year-book (or teacher's reflective practice journal)

K*   X parent and or teacher's observations on child's strength of character and needs.

Form I   X parent and or teacher's observations on child's strength of character and needs.

Form II   X

Form III   X Unclear how long practice continues, the eventual goal being self-evaluation and management, the student may begin to transition to a Student-Yearbook, Map of Mansoul, etc. at the beginning of form III with *Ourselves*, while parent continues private observations.

Form IV   X increasing self-evaluation and management with *Ourselves*.

Forms V, VI   X self-evaluation and management with *Ourselves* Bk. II.

Life

Student Year-book (also Motto Book)

K*

Form I

Form II   X copy mottoes in beautiful lettering—may also include copying/illuminating on beautiful paper.

Form III   X Choose and inscribe mottoes in beautiful lettering.

Form IV   X Choose and inscribe mottoes in beautiful lettering.

Forms V, VI   X Uncertain—No record

Life

Fortitude Book, Book of Heroes, etc.

K*

Form I

Form II

Form III

Form IV

Forms V, VI   X self-evaluation and management with Bk. II of *Ourselves*.

Life   X

Map of Mansoul (Mason likely didn't use actual map)

K*

Form I

Form II

Form III   X on-going student project—pictorial narration of Mansoul with *Ourselves* Bk. I.

Form IV   X on-going student project—pictorial narration of Mansoul with *Ourselves* Bk. I.

Forms V, VI

Life

Way of the Will Chart (Mason likely didn't use actual chart)

K*

Form I

Form II

Form III

Form IV

Forms V, VI   **X** For use with *Ourselves* in discussing the "Way of the Will" and upper Literature, History classes.

Life

Bible Notebook

K*

Form I   X uncertain, possibly contains drawings.

Form II   X uncertain, probably begins with written narration.

Form III   **X**

Form IV   **X**

Forms V, VI **X**

Life   **X**

Others

(Bible also belongs under this heading. See above.)

Timelines

K*   As readiness indicates–"Child's Own."

Form I   **X** "Child's Own"—family first, moving finally to local events.

Form II   **X** "Table of History" (20 columns) moving to "Stream of History" when ready.

Form III   **X** "Stream of History" added to & kept visible.

Form IV   **X** "Stream of History" added to & kept visible.

Forms V, VI **X** "Stream of History" added to & kept visible.

Life

History/Century Charts

K*

Form I

Form II

Form III   **X** Make a chart of the period studied, visible.

Form IV   **X** Make a chart of the period studied, visible.

Forms V, VI **X** Make a chart of the period studied, visible.

Life

Book of Centuries

K*	
Form I	
Form II	**X** Begin at age 10—Illustrate from all History studied during the term.
Form III	**X** Illustrate from all History studied during the term.
Form IV	**X** Illustrate from all History studied during the term.
Forms V, VI	**X** Illustrate from all History studied during the term.
Life	**X**

Calendar of Events

K*	
Form I	
Form II	.
Form III	**X** Read the daily news, keep a calendar of events & narrative poems on events that strike one.
Form IV	**X** Read the daily news, keep a calendar of events & narrative poems on events that strike one.
Forms V, VI	X uncertain if practice continues once habit of reading news and discussing is established.
Life	

Work of Our Hands

Music Notebook

K*	
Form I	Possibly simple copy work.
Form II	**X** Use uncertain, probably after year 4 "to produce sign and sound from a passage studied."
Form III	**X** to produce sign and sound from a passage studied."
Form IV	**X** to produce sign and sound from a passage studied."
Forms V, VI	**X to** produce sign and sound from a passage studied."
Life	

Enquire Within

K*	
Form I	
Form II	**X** Use uncertain, drawings & dictated notes could be gathered, but probably begins with strong written narration ability.
Form III	**X** Records "exactly how to do everything."
Form IV	**X** Records "exactly how to do everything."
Forms V, VI	**X** Records "exactly how to do everything."
Life	**X**

Fig.14 Forms of Vitality across the Years *(design Laurie Bestvater)* *formal classes begin at 6

Part Two

5

R.S.V.P. The Shape of Life

He openeth man's ear morning by morning,
to hear so much of the best as the man is able to hear.

– Charlotte Mason

Important lessons: look carefully; record what you see.
Find a way to make beauty necessary; find a way to make necessity beautiful."

– Anne Michaels

So why *do* keepers of notebooks keep them? To what siren call are they compelled to respond? It is a "why did the chicken cross the road?" question. Invariably, the explorations of notebook aficionados begin with this; Didion is not the first to wonder about the impulse of the Keeper, nor the last. Hannah Hinchman in her decades long inquiry into Keeping wonders about it, unsure if her nature walks led to her notebooks or the notebooks to the nature walks but convinced nonetheless of the numinous quality of Keeping: "There were rituals, enacted with earnestness. I didn't feel I had created them, but that they had existed for eons and I'd somehow become an initiate."[246] Mason is very familiar with these rituals and that Keepers are pilgrims who have stood with Socrates and others at the summit, beholding the wonder of an "examined life."

And like others in her genre, Hinchman is drawn to look to children when she associates attention with living with notebooks.

> What is it about the child's mind that allows it to register
> impressions with such clarity? We know the child hasn't a

> more sophisticated way of gathering information: it's the same fluid, haphazard process we use as adults. But our receptivity diminishes as we mature; we must channelize our lives to get along in the adult world. Before that channelizing begins, the child can linger in self-forgetfulness. She stands and gazes or listens and lives in the gazing or listening. There is nothing held back, she is all eyes and ears. Nor is she projecting anything, not generalizing or classifying. She's being impressed.
>
> How to invite that immersion, how to arrive at it more readily?[247]

How indeed? Is this not the learner that we long for in our classrooms, "nothing held back...all eyes and ears," "impressed?" Mason, the great observer of children, also asks and eventually answers, "how to arrive at it more readily." "Most Grown Men Lose the Habit of Observation" her heading announces.[248] This quality of being "all eyes and ears" is clearly a gift that children arrive with and which sadly they lose or have educated out of them. She notices that those grown-ups who manage to preserve it have "a certain freshness, gentleness and capacity of being pleased" like unto a child and she spends the rest of her life in the service of this Grand Invitation: "to be converted and become like children." (Matt. 18:3 New American Standard Bible) Mason confirms with educator and philosopher Kieran Egan that every child is born a poet, and ethicist Reinhold Niebuhr, "Every child is a born theologian." And she insists we offer the children in our care the means of "lingering in this self-forgetfulness" with these forms of vitality as a tangible means of grace.[249]

Notice she is after the self-forgetfulness natural to children; self is not the object.[250] As Keepers, Mason has in mind "resistant rearrangers" for a more splendid end: the discovery of what it is to be a flourishing human being, an adept noticer of Glory. We may not settle for a myopic view; "any effort which has self as an end is poor and narrow."[251] Even a brief survey of the literature of Keepers reveals that many do land on the wee island of self and never travel any farther abroad. Mason finds that a sad miscarriage of any serious formative enterprise. The examined life is only part of the story; Mason's practice does not bend toward that "morbid introspection."[252] She is *not* looking for beautiful notebooks housing a precious "History of Me;" her posture predates, and thankfully escapes, the chicken and egg debate over student self-esteem.

Jennifer New, in her study of Keepers, confesses that a large part of the modern practice is self-absorbed, that many of the hundreds of notebooks she surveyed "contain the emotional stuff of everyday life, a young woman's search for self: some whining and self-pity, a lot of fretting and occasional joy."[253] As Dr. Lynee Gaillent observes in her research on the role of the commonplace in teaching composition, self is a modern addition. "Writing texts advocating the use of commonplace books rarely include expressive writing assignments typically associated with modern journal keeping."[254] Mason's is always a focus greater than and outside of self. Self will be enlarged and known intimately in the careful listening and looking of the Keeper but along the way, as a byproduct and not as an end. The gifts of time, place, and relationship which are Mason's genius to protect call for these almost hidden postures known by philosophers and mystics alike to lead to wisdom.[255] She is always after the inner transformation that inoculates against "channelizing our lives to get along in the adult world," and all the passing of tests, making of careers, or the adulation of self that may involve.

This is a rather fine distinction as our tour through the gallery of notebooks has shown. We are not converging on the self but the heart; "we are educated by our desires." As the famous men and women Keepers we encountered in chapter one reveal, it is most often a deep longing of the heart that leads to the passionate embrace of and the consequent achievements in all fields: science, nature, exploration, art, and literature. And there is a mystery about this drive that remains undisclosed. In becoming intimate with these lives, Mason hopes her students will see in each notable, how "some living idea of God may arrest his Mind and stir up his Will to desire, intend, resolve," because those are the ultimate postures of a human fully alive.[256]

Mason is not pursuing achievement *per se*. Her education is an acknowledgement of the heart—a heart that is "made for and must have a God."[257] A child must have a clear sightline to Glory, and the notebooks are a means to invite this seeing. In a passage widely quoted in Mason circles but not widely enough in our No Child Left Behind culture, she is utterly clear:

Our aim in Education is to give a Full Life.
We begin to see what we want. Children make large demands upon us. We owe it to them to initiate an immense number of interests. "Thou hast set my feet in a

large room" should be the glad cry of every intelligent soul. Life should be all *living*, and not merely a tedious passing of time; not all doing or all feeling or all thinking—the strain would be too great—but all living; that is to say, we should be in touch wherever we go, whatever we hear, whatever we see, with some manner of vital interest. We cannot *give* the children these interests; we prefer that they should never say they have learned botany or conchology, geology or astronomy. **The question is not,—how much does the youth *know*? when he has finished his education—but how much does he *care*? and about how many orders of things does he care?** In fact, how large is the room in which he finds his feet set? and, therefore, how full is the life he has before him?[258] (emphasis mine)

Philosopher, James K.A. Smith in *Desiring the Kingdom* takes up the call for such a "re-visioning of education" in our day.

What if education, including higher education, is not primarily about the absorption of ideas and information, but about formation of hearts and desires? What if we began by appreciating how education not only gets into our head but also (and more fundamentally) grabs us by the gut—what the New Testament refers to as *Kardia*, 'the heart?' What if education was primarily concerned with shaping our hopes and passions—our visions of "the good life"—and not merely about the dissemination of data and information as inputs to our thinking? What if the primary work of education was the transforming of our imagination rather than the saturation of our intellect?" And what if this had as much to do with our bodies as with our minds? What if education wasn't first and foremost about what we know, but about what we love? [259]

"Studies serve for delight." Education is not about how much we know but how much we love and care.[260] What are our notebooks if not a means to return to all the things we love and care about? Such knowledge is the natural by-product of working with and not against the Natural Law of the learner. If we put the cart before the horse and seek only the knowledge and achievement without the caring, we may endanger both, participating in what Quentin Schultze aptly calls "informational promiscuity."[261] Armstrong notes that there is something terribly amiss when people like Bill Gates point to high school drop-out rates and remark that high school is "obsolete."[262] And yet delight seems an almost outlandish term in the serious world of school.

Most of us would agree that something has gone terribly wrong, but finding a way to "balance the power between the claims of body, mind and soul," is less likely to be a landing place than stepped up academics, more stringent rules, and knuckling down on a "new" curriculum.[263] Abbot and former headmaster of Genstal Abbey School in Ireland, Mark Hederman, defines the wrong as something ancient and persistent, a developmental process that culminated in the

> Scientific positivism (that) declared that there was nothing other than the real observable world and that we contained within ourselves the power to explain and to dominate this palpable reality. From this final triumph of reason we had reached our maturity. It had been necessary to pass from a mythological stage through a metaphysical stage to this ultimate and positive stage. For the intelligent adult, reason was lord. Nothing in reality could escape the penetration of logic. All could be reduced to principles, causes, reasons. Any other interpretations represent an infantile stage of humanity on its way towards the discovery of itself as sole interpreter of reality.[264]

It turns out we may have been asking the wrong questions, and in this post-Enlightenment culture it is extraordinarily easy to do, even for those of us who are compelled to a thorough search for an education true to the way things are.

~ ~ ~ ~ ~ ~ ~

In his quest to describe how we are formed and trace the causes of inner growth, Richard Foster, the well-known Quaker theologian, concludes with Mason that transformation is ultimately beyond our control, mysteriously brought about by the Holy Spirit. And yet he also isolates practices, long known by the Church as "means of grace," that somehow allow us to open ourselves to this growth.

> Is it not logical to conclude that we must wait for God to come and transform us? Strangely enough, the answer is no. The analysis is correct—human striving *is* insufficient and righteousness *is* a gift from God—but the conclusion is faulty. Happily there is something we can do. We do not need to be hung on the horns of the dilemma of either human works or idleness. God has given us the Disciplines of the spiritual life as a means of receiving his grace. The Disciplines allow us to place ourselves before God so he can transform us.[265]

Foster puts his finger on one of the both/and paradoxes described by Christianity and which Mason knows well: "happily, there is something we can do." As St. Augustine says, "We speak, but it is God who teaches." Mason scholar Benjamin Bernier points out that the Church of England and its calendar had a significant part in shaping the House of Education.[266] Charlotte Mason not only lived with these means of grace, she internalized them and brilliantly elucidated how they apply to education.[267] Apparently, Mason was much influenced by Church of Scotland minister, Alexander Whyte who "believed that education, high culture, and profound spirituality could not be divorced."[268] In fact, says Bernier, "our separation of sacred and secular knowledge prevents us from appreciating the importance of the sacramental harmony existing between matter and spirit underlying Mason's educational views."[269]

It *is* hard to capture in words at times, but with the Great Recognition Mason flings wide the doors of the classroom to the "spiritual" disciplines. Since a child is a whole person, indivisible, she will allow no difference between spiritual growth and any other; all education, "whether in Euclid, or grammar, or music, (is) a direct inspiration from the Holy Spirit, without any thought at all as to whether the person so inspired named himself by the name of God, or recognised whence his inspiration came."[270] Mason insists we are not thinking clearly when we divide education into "religious and secular" and maintains even the slightest equivocation in anthropology has immediate and serious repercussions.[271]

A man of our age, with its post-Enlightenment tendency to divide, Foster intuits what Smith, Schultze, and others are saying about needing a greater focus on the heart and virtue in education but seems to pull back ever so slightly with the phrase, "God has given us the disciplines of the spiritual life." Mason would contend that God has given us the disciplines of life. Period. These disciplines allow us to place our students before the divine Spirit who mysteriously transforms them.[272]

This explains why in *Ourselves* Mason puts public worship, private prayer, and reading good books on par.[273] Though not holding these things as salvific, she sees that "nothing speaks to us more directly from the Spirit of God than the best books of the best men"[274] While upholding the supremacy of scripture, "THE BOOK, <u>par excellence</u>,"[275] Mason's is a wide understanding of *Lectio Divina…"divine reading…*the traditional Benedictine practice of scriptural reading, meditation, and prayer intended to promote communion with God."[276] Foster simply calls it the discipline of study, and to be fair, like Mason, he does not limit such "spiritual" study solely to scripture either, remarking that "books are both verbal and non-verbal" and that we should read Great Works, "by men and women from many walks of life (since) many of these thinkers have unusual perception into the human condition."[277]

What has this to do with Mason's forms of vitality? I realize that for the sake of example I may have been expecting more of Foster than he set out to do in that passage. Mason herself uses the term, "spiritual life." I do not wish to dishonor his fine work in any way, but I think his slight equivocation does signal the schizophrenia with which our culture can approach a person and ultimately education. Or perhaps the equivocation is in us as readers; we can recognize the feast but stop short of Mason's sacramental insistence that we not divide "spiritual" from everything else and her radical call to include children at the table.

> We allow no separation to grow up between the intellectual and "spiritual" life of children, but teach them that the Divine Spirit has constant access to their spirits, and is their continual Helper in all the interests, duties and joys of life.[278]

Whatever the cause of the rift, understanding Mason's forms of vitality seems an educational healing of sorts, a way to sew up what has been divided—her notebooks can demonstrate that "the world and knowledge do not exist in sealed compartments."[279] Just as we cannot separate one subject rightly from another, we may not divide a person into his "parts" and educate each in isolation. "The powers of Mansoul are many, but they are one."[280]

In the popular novel, *The Guernsey Literary and Potato Peel Pie Society,* one of the characters says,

> That's what I love about reading: one tiny thing will interest you in a book, and that tiny thing will lead you onto another book, and another bit there will lead you onto a third book. It's geometrically progressive—all with no end in sight, and for no other reason than sheer enjoyment.

Mason's students recognize this winding path; all is connected, and all is relationship.[281] No separation has been allowed to grow up. The forms of vitality have an inherent potential to invite and safeguard this wholeness as they cross disciplines. They become the means of grace in education. "Traditionally, *Lectio Divina* has four separate steps: *read, meditate, pray,* and *contemplate.*"[282] If, as cultural critics like Postman and Schulze contend, the materialism, behaviorism, and scientism of the last hundred years have often given us ways in education that are counter to our message of the "whole child," to the point that often we cannot even see the disconnect, in becoming Keepers we begin to restore our vision.[283] We noted earlier the Natural Law and the anthropology upon which Mason's pedagogy is constructed, but I hope it is becoming clear that its synergy and unity must logically find their outworking in these paper graces—the notebooks call for the reading, meditating, praying, and contemplation that lead to true education. Mason, addressing her House of Education students, recommended meditation repeatedly, for apprehending thoughts of God and as worthy practice in other subjects. "It is told that Mr. Romaines once asked Darwin to advise him as to the best course to take in the pursuit of science. The answer of the elder scientist was, 'meditate.' "[284] It seems almost silly in our modern ear. But we discount Mason's trust in these postures to our peril; "the future of the man or woman depends very largely on the store of real knowledge gathered, and the habits of intelligent observation acquired by the child."[285] We need the living page.

Keeping Imagination and Attention

What we become keepers of determines whom we become. As we keep the living page, we keep imagination and attention and, ultimately, safeguard the personhood of children. Mason demonstrates that children are born storytellers and poets and that it is in acting on living ideas with their own minds that children grow. The blank page countenances this relationship to the material and respects personhood, mind, and creativity. On the other hand, if I structure your page with blanks to be filled or draw the diagram for you to label, or photocopy the map, I rob you of this work of the mind and ultimately depress your ability to imagine and respond for yourself. The blank page whispers "once upon a time…" and the child supplies the rest in words and symbols fresh from his mind and heart.[286] The page becomes a live thing, the shape of his own unique essence, a personal response to the Grand Invitation.

Mason would say imagination and metaphor are crucial in education because of how we are made, that humans are image bearers of a creative and Word-speaking God. We need not share her faith perspective to arrive at the conclusion that children need these ways of approach, however. Not only do we come to understand the need for metaphor and imagination in a careful observation of children, we see it readily in societies down through time: after food and shelter needs are met, humankind invariably turns to story and creativity to comprehend the Perennial Questions: Who are we? Why are we here? What are good and evil? What happens after we die? and What can life mean? Obviously, I am not suggesting "fine art" as we know it in the West has always existed, but as philosopher and Pulitzer prize winning author Marilynne Robinson confirms in her essay, "Freedom of Thought," man is a maker and in approaching the existential questions, liturgy, dance, and symbol have always existed in human culture in some form and must be accounted for. [287]

Contemplating the sad effects of the previous century's Industrial Revolution, Mason refuses to back down. These are issues for all peoples and creeds; humans are meaning-makers that require more than just information. A full human life requires the intact imagination that her method preserves. As Calvin Seerveld, distinguished professor of philosophical aesthetics, outlines below, there is a stratum of truth beyond fact that all genuine approaches to education must comprehend:

What Gerald Manley Hopkins called the inscape of things—that suggestive shape of poplar leaves falling like echoes against a leaden sky or the shapely-patterned movement of mackerel flip-flopping in the bottom of a row-boat—points to the fact that fish, trees, and air can function as objects of aesthetic awareness because everything in creation has a dimension of nuancefulness. It takes aesthetic sense that goes beyond simple perception and even empathy to pick up and view those quirks as noteworthy glories pregnant with similarities that one wants to notice but would not want to spoil by processing conceptually.

It changes your walk down the street (if one *walks* down a street) to pick out the quilt of different greens in trees, shrubs and grasses in spring. [288]

Mason's student *does* walk down the street and what is more, she knows her Book of Firsts is waiting to receive the "noteworthy glories." Her dry brush painting of a carefully chosen specimen each week of her school life in her nature notebook (accomplished often without the manufactured green provided in her paint box!) has trained her eye to the myriad personalities of green. Her current historical fiction describing the settling of the colonies has awakened her mind's eye to quilts pieced carefully from garments that cannot be persuaded to clothe one more child and so necessary to keeping off the snow that blows in at the chinks in the cabin walls and sifts over sleeping heads in the night. Fish in boat bottoms already signify feasting while they run and drying for the time when they do not, and because of the blank page of her narration journal, the nuancefulness of her walk does not escape her.

~ ~ ~ ~ ~ ~ ~

I love this coined word of Seerveld's; I think G. M. Hopkin's "inscape" and Seerveld's "nuancefulness" begin to get at what Mason meant by "knowing glory." I think many of us become educators because of our own inklings of "nuancefulness;" we believe that education should change how one walks down the street. We want students who are curious and alert, ready for each particular daily encounter and how it relates to every other with the ability to see and to connect. Yet, as we saw, a subtle slip in our definition of the person and our early enthusiasm for teaching can be dulled inadvertently by adopting the typical mixture of behavioristic techniques and even near acrobatics that we are told will "work" on our students. Marian Ney calls this divided and divisive hodge-podge phenomenon educational "impedimenta."

> Research is extensive, heavily subsidized, and, ultimately, presents little unity. The conclusions reached by one group usually contradict those of another. A problem arises when the public schools grab at one or another thesis and throw their power into inflicting this latest fad upon the already-confused teachers and pupils.[289]

I hope it is evident by now that this is *not* what Mason is doing with her use of notebooks. If one thing is apparent from the overview I am attempting, I hope it is the unity of Mason's approach. We can scarcely fathom how the practice *in its totality* supports the student's formation and fullness of life. One cannot faddishly add a nature notebook to an already full and disjointed school day and expect the outcomes the P.N.E.U. saw.[290] All of Mason's practices appear to be carefully considered for their ability to nurture what the child already has within him, including imagination, and one suspects the effect of their synergy is nothing short of remarkable.[291]

That said, it should hearten us that current neuroscience often supports Mason's perceptions about metaphor and imagination. Mason is expressing, ahead of the many who have come to bemoan the effects of our overdependence on rationalism and scientism, that we must be Keepers of imagination.[292] Mike Metzger, founder of the think-tank, The Clapham Institute, grapples with such Post-Enlightenment effects every day and notes that "according to neuroimaging, making sense of the world is a function of the brain's right hemisphere." Metzger suggests we adopt the position of C.S. Lewis in his essay, " 'Bluspels and Flalansferes.' In it, he wrote, 'All our truth, or all but a few fragments, is won by metaphor.' Metaphor is a right hemisphere function. It's *imagination.* Lewis believed imagination precedes reason."[293]

It is no small irony that Science is now actually seeing what, Metzger points out, Einstein already knew, that the human brain is made to deal with images and metaphors and not just propositions. It seems that to keep the blank page, "formless and void," is to work in concert with the natural laws of who we are as humans. If we scan the list of notebooks Mason proposes, we can see her wonderful intuition in balancing right and left brain support; the blank page welcomes both drawing, a right brain function, and writing, a left brain one. Far from being obsolete, Mason's paper postures appear to be extraordinarily useful—essential even.

Although Mason has children enjoying words and the literary in every possible configuration, much of the student's daily work deals in image and metaphor. If we consider the whole array of notebooks, we see many venues for image and education of the hand in a delightful variety of mediums: dry brush watercolors in the Nature Notebooks, pen and ink drawing in the Book of Centuries, calligraphy and graphic design in the Commonplace and copy work, simple pencil sketches of maps, diagrammed instructions in the Enquire Within, the quick charcoal narrations of picture study, and the routine of musical notation. Clearly, in this largely left-brain culture, Mason offers a more balanced approach even within the notebooks.[294]

~~~~~~~

Imagination and attention are inseparable in the notebook practice. Of all the ways of welcoming personality, imagination, and metaphor noted above, we could list in equal number the ways the notebooks cater to attending. Nuancefulness is a helpful word. To write a simple narration, as anyone who has tried it knows, takes all our powers of attention and a type of listening beyond what most of us accomplish with even our most intimate loved ones. To get the exact shade of a flower in our paints, to copy a passage with all the spelling and punctuation marks, to memorize a painting in a few short minutes to tell or sketch it back, to observe an artifact and reproduce it in our Book of Centuries, to walk such that we see the tips of the snowdrops that were not there yesterday poke above the lawn grasses for the Book of Firsts, to attend to the rolling of the croissant, so that we can write the instructions with diagrams later in our Enquire Within, are all attending. We are being coached to see with the inner eye of imagination.

Contrary to the stereotype of the imagining child being a dreamer who must be recalled to his task constantly, Mason knows allowing a child full scope for his imagination actually superintends the focused attention she seeks. The two capacities work in tandem, and imagination and attention aid and abet each other in the notebooks, as in life. It is the child whose imagination has been suppressed that is disinterested and apathetic, says professor Vigen Guroian.[295] And naturally, disinterest and apathy cannot lead to the care and full living Mason covets for her students. In fact, a lively imagination is perhaps one of the most important elements in our moral development. As Mason emphasized and now the likes of Guroian and Sir Ken Robinson campaign, there is an intimate relationship between imagination and empathy.[296] How can I see what you are suffering if I cannot imagine your conditions and your pain? If empathy is one of the distinctives of human beings as Robinson says it is, an education for humans cannot afford to downplay the role of creativity and imagination. Attending, too, makes us more human and alive to the other; how can I possibly be compassionate if I have not paid attention to those who lie at the side of the road of my life?[297]

~ ~ ~ ~ ~ ~ ~

Certainly it is a relief in our day to hear more voices calling for right-brained support—and Mason's notebooks are a real step in that direction—but it is also crucial to realize that she sees so much more than "soft skills" at stake here. The forms of vitality are not just expedient classroom tools that work with the nature of the student and reality and hence lead to "better" outcomes; they support a moral imperative. Attention and imagination will succor virtuous behavior, but even that is too shallow a goal for Mason. She is not after good behavior per se; perhaps character is a word that will barely carry the import of what she envisions. For her, "to will" or to choose is the ultimate mark of a human, and Mason's educational efforts are designed to midwife the child's recognition that "a king is not a king unless he reigns and a man is less than a man unless he wills."[298] If to choose is the essence of our humanity, our practice *must* strengthen attention and imagination through the living page in order to emancipate the child's ability to accept or reject ideas.[299] We scaffold with these various notebooks because "attention is the first step towards willing"[300] and imagination considers the results of that willing. "It is only as we have it in us to let a person or a cause fill the whole stage of the mind, to the exclusion of self-occupation, that we are capable of large-hearted action on behalf of that person or cause."[301]

Keeping Time

Mason's notebooks also make us keepers of time in surprising ways. They teach us very tangibly to be "clock wise"[302] along with cultural critics like

Quentin Schultze, Neil Postman, Wendell Berry, Calvin Seerveld, and others who are seeing that "today, we increasingly assume that doing things quickly and effectively is more important than doing them carefully, thoughtfully, and ethically."[303] Nothing about the forms of vitality promotes quickness and efficiency, as we usually understand those terms. It may take several 20-minute sessions to draw a map of a battle or a student's own street when it would be much quicker to photocopy that for the student and test him on his labeling next week. One could cover much more ground with a natural history textbook than ever will be evident in a Nature Notebook added to "by the way," an entry at a time, week on week. The Book of Centuries may never contain a full century's content; its 100 spots for happenings and its one page for the careful drawing of artifacts cannot possibly contain "it all" and may take a lifetime to fill. Writing a passage by hand into a beautiful notebook takes more time and effort than snapping a photo of it with my smartphone. An Enquire Within that I write for myself seems almost pointless when I can Google any recipe or procedure and print the instructions in a matter of seconds.[304] In standard parlance, the notebooks are not "effective" for the compiling of information, the teacher's need to "get something done," or for assessing the content acquired by any one student.

But let us reconsider what effectiveness means, and the brilliance of these living pages lights up. The notebooks suggest by their very presence a rhythm of "doing things carefully and thoughtfully" that we are unwittingly hungry for. Unlike typical schoolhouse practices, the child lives with her notebooks in an ongoing way, the rhythms of use ebbing and flowing with the terms, and even years. The Three Pillars, especially, are companions over a lifetime, roving with the students in and out of interests and periods of growth. Looking back at one's pages one can see new gifts unfolding, certain traits becoming habitual, and personality emerging. One's notebooks become treasured friends, offering a conversation about being in the world where even our missteps are instructive.[305] They are effective and affective in the deepest sense. In a typical classroom, work rarely lasts a term before being discarded, let alone years.

A child under this method has a pace set for life with his notebooks. Some books fill up quickly; others have just a few entries per season. He sees that life is not neatly packaged but grows in fits and starts, but steadily. The forms of vitality act as brakes to the runaway train of consumption to which liberal arts education can fall prey.[306] There are only so many passages one's hand can copy in a day, only so many paintings one can absorb and narrate. A song learned by heart, a recipe demonstrated, tasted, revised, and drawn takes time, sets a time, keeps time to a human scale. One is not permitted to go "hog wild" with the whole feast. The notebooks keep us from becoming gluttonous consumers of Glory. There will be more tomorrow, like manna. One thinks of Wendell Berry's incisive quip, "think little." [307] Here is the principle of the mustard seed; though the smallest of all seeds, it grows the largest plant. In adding to our notebooks day by day, in keeping their implicit clock, we get a rhythm inside ourselves that may very well be revolutionary. As Schultz forecasts, "if we are not able to slow down enough to rediscover moral wisdom, our high-tech endeavors will create ever more diversionary noise, resulting in thinner lives." [308] With Mason we are refusing the mile wide, inch deep educational status quo for the deeply rooted affection and care of a simple and measured approach. Big and fast and lots are not the only way; "Less is truly more!" the notebooks cry.

~ ~ ~ ~ ~ ~ ~

I have to share a story about a "rhythm inside ourselves." My daughter teaches music. I've watched her; she glows as she interacts with her students, and I have often wondered how learning Mason "from the underside," as a student and a recipient of these deep and timeful practices rather than from the top down of reading the theory, like her mother, would feel. In some ways, not being "brought up" under Mason's work myself and understanding her but little in the early days, Sarah was a bit of an experiment (and she doesn't mind my saying that). While I was working on this book, she shared the following episode that really helped to bring home the importance of Mason's fight against "thin lives:"

> Tonight I told a nine-year-old girl to listen to her foot tapping in her piano lesson and to imagine it instead in her heart. She knew exactly what I meant and finished my sentence for me: "You mean, like a heart-tap?" "Yes, that's exactly what I mean,"I told her. "You feel your foot, and then when I ask you to play while imagining the foot-tap instead of letting your foot do it, what happens? You saw; your head taps instead! because you have so much rhythm inside your body that it has to come out somewhere! But if

you listen to your foot or your head really carefully, you'll discover that you have that rhythm in your body **everywhere** and you'll be able to find it just by listening to your arm or your nose. Because it's all the same, you see, and it's everywhere once you have learned to listen for what it really sounds like, and you can always find it in your heart."

And d---ed if she didn't get the rhythm perfect for the rest of the night. [309]

My daughter hasn't had any education courses. She has heard me, probably ad nausea, talk about Mason, but her *experience* of the pedagogy has sunk in deeply, it seems to me. Several "Mason" things appear in this short passage that tell me that *the way* we spend time with children really matters. Many children have troubles with their piano teachers as they learn the difficult task of right hand and left hand doing different things whilst their brain is meant to be counting. But somehow Sarah knows she is with this student and for now, she is the only student with this problem and approaches respectfully. She doesn't remind, roll her eyes, let out an exasperated sigh, utter, "how many times have I told you?" or offer candy or stickers to the child in order to get her to stop what can only be described as a constant irritation if you are a piano teacher. She breaks from what is the perceived lesson, the "getting through" the piece, to have the learning moment that the child has shown her she needs. She clearly has a tender relationship with her, though I know she has a full studio and must have many students. And Sarah has been watching her student; she has seen her struggle to keep the foot still only to have the head bob, and she offers a view to the next handhold. She stands beside, as a co-learner, someone who has been through the toe-tapping difficulty herself. She is not talking down, but simply and respectfully calls on the child's imagination, and asks her to see what is really there. The child does the rest.

It did this mother's heart proud to hear it, but that's not why I retell this story. I tell it because even my shambling efforts in the direction Mason was pointing were somehow enough for some deep sense of the proper use of time and place and relationship to take root in the next generation of teacher without, it seems, her even knowing it. And this is not to say that one must be a Mason teacher in order to be of such use to a student. Sarah's Suzuki teachers had similar practices; all good teachers do these things. That was the gist of Mason's message: There are ways to approach persons that are always respectful, always timeful, always rich relationally. I only offer this anecdote because there were so many typical ways Sarah might have handled this student and didn't, and it seemed remarkable that she was that in sync with Mason's postures without any education "training." Since that night, I have wondered, how did she know that the Chopin, excellent though the piece was, was not the most important thing, unless she had Mason's rhythm inside herself?

~~~~~~~

Embedded in these paper postures are also the undeniable patterns of the seasons and the Church calendar. In a sense, they are the timepieces: "Last year at this time I was reading…." "Two springs ago, the daffodils were up by Easter." "My copybook began with cursive so large, and now my penmanship is rather half as big." "Oh, there is the poem I loved most when I was six; can I still say it?" It may not be readily apparent, but it is an effective approach; the things that do get collected, sometimes haltingly, on these pages are real connections and represent deep relationship—slowly and certainly the child is "being built up from within." The notebooks bear witness that true formation cannot be hurried.[310] In Schultze's terms, Keeping is a way of "doing things ethically;" such caring and choosing as Mason is proposing takes time.

Again there is science to support. In his 2012 examination of decision-making called *Wait*, Frank Partnoy, "as any good lawyer would,"[311] carefully delineates what we know about the human ability to choose. He says time is essential to that unique capacity that philosophers like Viktor Frankl and Francis Schaeffer have pointed to as *the* fundamental human characteristic, our ability to choose.[312] Partnoy confirms that new strides in brain, and surprisingly, heart, science have led "many scientists (to) say the key aptitude that distinguishes human beings from animals is our superior ability to think about the future."[313] Mason calls this capacity "the Way of the Will," and she arrives at Partnoy's conclusion a century before he does: "*the way of the will is a slow way.*"[314](emphasis mine) Accordingly, she structures all of her method and curriculum to provide for this moral education, the strengthening of the human muscle known as will, what Partnoy would call decision-making.

So Mason's instinctual reliance on the seasons, liturgy, Church year, a very defined classroom schedule, and ultimately the notebooks, is to preserve the human-paced and simple, and gently helps us learn to keep time. As we face a world she could never have imagined that speeds dizzily by, it is a reassurance to see her common sense wisdom echoing through the data: we must slow down. Asserting that Canadian author and researcher Malcolm Gladwell's famous notions about images and "thin-slicing" in *Blink* reveal only part of the story of how our minds work, Partnoy argues that while we are human persons with amazing mental capacities, time is an essential element for being fully human choosers.

> The essence of my case is this: given the fast pace of modern life, most of us tend to react too quickly. We don't or can't, take enough time to think about the increasingly complex timing challenges we face. Technology surrounds us, speeding us up. We feel its crush every day, both at work and at home. Yet the best time managers are comfortable pausing for as long as necessary before they act, even in the face of the most pressing decisions. Some seem to slow down time. For good decision makers, time is more flexible than a metronome or atomic clock.[315]

~~~~~~~

All kinds of exciting research come to light every day. Mason helps us know what to do with the "new" data. As every scientist knows or should, data requires a set of glasses with which to view the spectacle. Partnoy cites another "so that" story in connection with a study done by Stanford University that tested preschoolers for their waiting (will) power. The children were offered one marshmallow right now and two marshmallows in 15 minutes and had to choose. Those who had strengthened that will muscle to the point of being able to wait for two marshmallows were consistently the better adjusted and higher achieving students later in life. In our culture's usual mania for marks and achievement however, parents who heard about the study started tinkering and anxiously testing their children's will power. Partnoy notes the irony of a school that even tried to teach this "skill" externally by having t-shirts printed admonishing, "Don't Eat the Marshmallow!"[316]

Mason draws us again to the person; "They are yet in the outer darkness of those who believe that 'to get on' is the chief thing in life."[317] Transformation does not come, nor is character built, by slogans or circus tricks. Understanding that the will is the prime lever of character, Mason has a considered, calm, and careful way to strengthen persons in their choosing and thinking based on an sophisticated understanding of "the way of the will" and "the way of reason." Partnoy himself notes that achievement cannot be controlled quite as those marshmallow-wielding parents had hoped. Ethical questions aside, and consistent with Mason's assertion that education is one third atmosphere, giving our students time may be one of the few elements of their learning within our power.

~~~~~~~~

We ought not look down on those parents; it is very easy to become enthralled by outcomes. Though spiffy academic results are not Mason's goal, they are a by-product of working with the principles she expounds. A P.N.E.U. examiner and critic once noticed in marking Mason's students' work that "the unsatisfactory (exam) papers are about at the rate of 1%."[318] Echoing her notion of "masterly inactivity," Partnoy also records that some of the best (most satisfying to work for and the most "successful") companies make sure their employees have 15% of their time to do what they choose.[319] Quoting Steven Johnson in *Where Good Ideas come From*, Partnoy points out that the Eureka moment is an anomaly—most innovations take time.[320] A lot of the most successful "big ideas" began in something as seemingly innocuous as play when their discoverers "were children, building the creative base for later insights."[321] As we saw with our consideration of the big name Keepers in chapter one, Science is confirming that there is an "off the clock" story, a living in "event time"[322] rather than clock time that is necessary for us to do our best thinking and deciding. Mason perceives that it is the "resistant rearrangers" who are most likely to be the innovators because they are (still) thinking like children. Partnoy is almost wistful.

> Somewhere out there is a kid thinking about an idea that might ultimately lead to a discovery as important as gravity or oxygen, or something as routinely ubiquitous as the Post-It. Right now, the idea behind that discovery is unformed, a dim thought in the back of this child's mind as she plays with a video game, observes her family's dog, or rebuilds a broken toy. If the discovery comes, it will not

be a light bulb suddenly going on. It will be the culmina-
tion of a decades-long process.[323]

We need the ways Mason proposes of ensuring this timefulness[324] and out of the box thinking not because it leads to more successful students and schools but because it is essential to our humanness and life's ultimate questions.[325] Rather than hop on the bandwagon to test what our children do with a marshmallow, Mason suggests we offer the blank page, which secures personhood by slowing us down, causing us to reflect, choose, sort, and ruminate. Being built up over time as we are, the notebooks innately support the kind of "decades long" connection and meditation that lead to profound creativity and innovation. As one inveterate Keeper affirms, we learn a discipline from our books; "they build a very palpable momentum."[326] We keep time with them.

Keeping Place

Our notebooks also connect us extraordinarily to place. Hinchman speaks eloquently about notebooks sharpening the ability to "really know the place you live," both the human and the natural environment.[327] She describes how on moving to a new community, her habit of keeping a notebook quickly rooted her. "In the evenings after work I would change into a summer dress and ride my bike to a café..." to observe and draw.[328] She not only got a sense of the local culture by practicing this ritual but was led by it to thinking about "deep ecology;" she contends that one's noticing leads to the reverent care of what one perceives to be one's home.

Invariably, Keepers testify that the capacity to really see one's own place changes how one looks at everything else. Professor Gary Brown notes that photos taken during travel require only a few seconds of attention as opposed to the time spent in careful looking and drawing required by a travel journal. He has filled over 400 sketch books with such drawings on his many journeys and says his notebook "is (his) secret friend, enemy, counselor, definitely (his) map and at times a thief...It sharpens you, your dreams, and your eyes stay wide as a child's."[329]

Ever seeking this childlikeness, Mason assuages her concern that "geography not be utilitarian," that all the child's experience of place (including science) keep its "mystery and beauty."[330] Somewhere the magic dance of the Keeper dawns on her. Perhaps on all those long walks in the Shires that led to *The Ambleside Geographies*, she saw that the notebook invites the seeing and the seeing then strengthens the notebook habit, rootedness and caring even further. Carol Beckwith, author of ten books on Africa, observes that her travel notebooks have this magical life of their own, *"they're living things, they need to grow."*[331] (emphasis mine)

~ ~ ~ ~ ~ ~ ~

In today's climate especially, with champions like Barry Lopez and Wendell Berry admonishing from the sidelines about our use and abuse of land, it seems very *avant garde* of Mason to warn against "using" land for our own purposes and profit.[332] But she does; and she adopts the various notebooks as practical insurance that her students will not become what Wendell Berry calls, "viewers of views," ubiquitous tourists snapping photos for their collections and never truly seeing or experiencing a place.[333] The capacity of the child to wonder and admire is protected by the Keeper's stance and Mason's commitment that he shall continue to be "awestruck."[334]

> He should be able to discriminate colours and shades of colours; relative degrees of heat in woolen, wood, iron, marble, ice; should learn the use of the thermometer; should discriminate objects according to their degrees of hardness; should have a cultivated eye and touch for texture; should, in fact, be able to get as much information about an object from a few minutes' study as to its form, colour, texture, size, weight, qualities, parts, characteristics, as he could learn out of many pages of a printed book.[335]

So the Enquire Within, for example, goes far beyond the students' need to know how to do certain practical things. Through it, Mason is solicitous to preserve the "education of the hand," the value of *things,* and thus place, in education.[336] The rhythms of housekeeping and practical tasks which are the daily habits of a well-ordered home (or school) grow the life-giving atmosphere she cherishes. Rootedness and stability result as everyone has a role in carrying out the daily-ness of life. And because personality is involved, this notebook is much more than a Wikipedia-type recitation. It has little to do with content and thus, Google cannot replace it. As author Rumer Godden, (herself a P.N.E.U parent in the early 1940's) conveys irresistibly in her story of a Cornwall manor house, *China Court*, work goes on, the same and yet never the same, each task valuable and formative with its "own little wrinkles" and the personality of the workman inherent.[337] The house or task may change hands, but always an atmosphere is being organically grown and maintained. Such a notebook preserves the awareness that it is always the embodied person who puts his hand to the task.

> Hands to direct, to sign letters and write checks for bills, to put a latchkey in the lock and bolt the doors at night. Other hands that hold keys too, but household keys; write notes that are dispatched, make pothooks in the top lines of copybooks, and pencil verses on canvas for samplers. These hands often write recipes: 'Our apple jelly with lavender and rosemary flavoring.' 'Our duck with cherries,' 'Our velvet cream.' The recipe book is still in the kitchen and Tracy's Great-great-grandmother Adza's velvet cream is still made on rare and especial occasions. These ladylike hands sew and knit; garden-but in gloves-play whist, leave cards, rub ointment on bruises; smooth hair back from hot foreheads, spank. There are younger, slimmer hands that embroider and do the flowers, play the piano, cut the pages of novels, sketch- 'and twiddle their thumbs'… There are small hands, very often dirty, that pry and poke into cupboards, work baskets, jam pots; make mud pies and cut out paper dolls; play cat's cradle and conkers, marbles, spillikins, Snap, Happy Families, and Monopoly— no, not Monopoly, for no one has played games in China Court for a long time and Monopoly is almost modern. There are humbler deft hands that sweep and dust, wash china and clothes and linen; iron, mend, sew, cook, bake, make fires and beds, sound gongs, carry trays; and rougher hands still that chop wood, clean shoes, groom, dig, wash the motorcar, mow the lawn, "but all our hands," says Mrs. Quin. "All belonging." And Tracy gives a sigh of content.[338]

Upholding the blank page repels and replaces the bewildered "book-learning" of the European model Mason decries and provides for a much more experiential and embodied culture than is typically understood by a "liberal education."[339] She admires the "education" of the North American Indian in this regard and seeks to fine-tune all the senses and the honoring of one's surroundings from that example. The forms of vitality are there summoning these observations and descriptions, working in concert with science done "by the way" and "within a walking radius of home" to create an education of deep placefulness.[340]

~ ~ ~ ~ ~ ~ ~

Berry is known for exalting over the importance of knowing one place well, and the following passage is rife with many of the qualities Mason is hoping to nurture in her students:

> In my teens, when I was away at school, I could comfort myself by recalling in intricate detail the fields I had worked and played in, and hunted over, and ridden through on horseback—and that were richly associated in my mind with people and with stories. I could recall even the casual locations of certain small rocks. I could recall the look of a hundred different kinds of daylight on all those places, the look of animals grazing over them, the postures and attitudes and movements of the men who worked in them, the quality of the grass and the crops that had grown on them. I had come to be aware of it as one is aware of one's body; it was present to me whether I thought of it or not.

Certainly, the Book of Firsts and the Nature Notebook are at the fore of this kind of noticing and relationship. The regular drawing and description that these notebooks want stimulate more careful seeing and the intimacy he describes. Yet Berry's connection alludes to the role of Mason's other notebooks as well when he links place with "people and stories."

> When I have thought of the welfare of the earth, the problems of its health and preservation, the care of its life, I have had this place before me, the part representing the whole more vividly and accurately, making clear and more pressing demands than *any idea* of the whole. When I have

thought of kindness or cruelty, weariness or exuberance, devotion or betrayal, carelessness or care, doggedness or awkwardness or grace, I have had in my mind's eye the men and women of this place, their faces and gestures and movements. [341]

The Book of Centuries and Commonplace serve to recognize the human geography, "the men and women of this place," that the children reading history and using their books to explore local artifacts will encounter. What "blood cries out from each corner of our school's street?"[342] "Which battles have been fought here?" "Who lived here first and from whence did they come?" "What buildings were here and are here now?" are all questions flowing from the use of living texts and the living pages of the notebooks which function as a corrective to utility.

Utility would adopt the notebooks in order *to make* environmentalists, (or good housekeepers or historians), another end-gaining, or "so that" position. There is always that danger; safety lies in asking, "how much does the student care?" Mason has always the Larger Room in view. Placefulness is an emphasis because persons need to care for each other and for the creation, to have meaningful work and a place to call home. Noticers and not "viewers of views" are more likely to care and to understand the stakes when decisions that affect our human and natural environments need to be taken. Berry and Mason would argue that Keepers find their place in the community more naturally because they have been nurtured in relationship and know the part intimately; they do not begin with the abstract idea of the whole. This is the genius of the notebooks. Even something as seemingly unconnected as the "Fortitude Journal," used in conjunction with *Ourselves* to give the student "a ground plan of human nature," is put to work to preserve the "world so full of beauty" by encouraging both self-awareness and other centeredness in its Keeper.[343] The passion and devotion of an environmentalist or homemaker or historian grow from this gentle keeping of Place—a grounded education with home as a touch point for all the large issues of life, but only through the intimate relationship, the love, that Berry describes. Again, Mason's postures originate from her understanding of a person. As humans, each of us starts with a home and the question, "where am I?" She hopes, by becoming Keepers, we arrive more readily at the answer, "here I am, send me."[344]

Keeping Relationships

Much of the current excitement about Mason's relational education has centered on the rich feast of ideas—great artists, writers, scientists and explorers the students are offered. Each child is meant to grow in Knowledge of God, Knowledge of Man, and Knowledge of the Universe through immediate and person-to-person contact because "a human being is born with a desire to know much about an enormous number of subjects."[345] That is well and good; it is a necessary amendment in our day of teaching to the test, to offer a truly liberal education to all. Academics are beginning to rally around the importance of narration and its fundamental role in this pedagogy. There also seems to be a trend within the movement to turn our attention now to the nuts and bolts of the practice of "masterly inactivity" with Mason retreats and "immersions" taking the foreground to allow people to experience this unique method as opposed to conferences of speakers telling us about it. What has yet to come into focus is the way this distinctive syllabus and method are sustained by the various paper postures Mason proposes. If the trinity of the Mason classroom is the rich curriculum plus the habit of narration and the teacher's "fine art of standing aside," the notebooks are the liturgy that invokes the formation and frames the student's encounter with Glory.

The wealth of relationships in her signature curriculum is requisite because "great ideas lead to great ends."[346] She is, after all, proposing an education of character, a "way to make great men." But I think the emphasis lies on the word "men" here and not on "great."[347] We are not in her classrooms to acquire The List of Great Books, rather we are looking to be changed, to become more human.

> We know that a great idea seizes hold of a man, has power to modify the tissues of the material organ by means of which he thinks, has power to alter the whole course of his life. Many a man can put his finger on the moment of his inception of that idea which made him a poet or a painter or a philanthropist.[348]

It is essential to grasp what Mason means by a great man and a good education if we are to comprehend the immense value of the invocation of the notebooks. It is a vision Schulz puts his finger on; "we need moral wisdom—the capacity to recognize what is intrinsically good and right, what is worth knowing and remembering, and how to use it wisely, if at all. Without such insight, we will discover that greater quantities of information become more of a curse than a blessing."[349] Mason would have us become people of character whose "observations are worth heeding." so that we can participate in the awakening of others to a life full of attention and gratitude.[350]

> Education must be in touch with Life. We must learn what we *desire to know*. Nobody talks to his friend about 'stinks,' about the niceties of Greek accents, nor, unless the two be mathematicians, about surds. But, when Jupiter is regnant, how good to tell and to learn! What a welcome companion is he who can distinguish between songs that differ in the vespers of the birds! How grateful the company of the reader of history who brings forward parallels to episodes in the Great War! We are apt to work for one thing in the hope that we shall get another and a very different thing; we don't. If we work for public examinations the questions in which must be of a narrow academic cast, we get a narrow, accurate, somewhat sterile type of mind. We reap as we have sown.[351]

Mason is *always* sowing for relationship: if there is a "so that" to her pedagogy, it is not the perfect SAT or the shining career, or even the heroic deed, but always relationship and care of the other: "lowly living, service and suffering."[352] She is with Frankl when he says, "being human always points, and is directed, to something or someone, other than oneself—be it a meaning to fulfill or another human being to encounter. The more one forgets himself—by giving himself to a cause to serve or another person to love—the more human he is."[353]

It is hard to imagine how Mason could have anticipated the things science is now discovering through advanced technologies if she had not built her method on a true conception of the human person. For instance, Psychologist and Stanford lecturer, Dr. Kelly McDonigal documents the importance of meditation.

> Neuroscientists have discovered that when you ask the brain to meditate, it gets better not just at meditating, but at a wide range of self-control skills, including attention, focus, stress management, impulse control, and self aware-ness. People who meditate regularly aren't just better at these things. Over time, their brains become finely tuned willpower machines.[354]

Mason wouldn't use the word "machines" but she would affirm the "Way of the Will" as upheld here and its importance in becoming more human.

Psychology professor Barbara Fredrickson recently described for the New York Times the physical changes that occur in a learner when daily interactions with others are warmer and more frequent. One might have anticipated changes in brain activity, but the startling results were that increasing positive relational encounters also impacted vagal tone, the heart. Fredrickson explains that the vagus nerve connects our hearts and brains and that scientists have discovered that it is plastic and influenced by social interaction. This is important since the vagus nerve is responsible for many health factors.

> In short, the more attuned to others you become, the healthier you become, and vice versa. This mutual influ-ence also explains how a lack of positive social contact diminishes people. Your heart's capacity for friendship also obeys the biological law of "use it or lose it." If you don't regularly exercise your ability to connect face to face, you'll eventually find yourself lacking some of the basic biologi-cal capacity to do so.[355]

We are literally and physically changed by our relationships; failing to account for relationship in education may actually result in "hard-hearted" or perhaps we should say, less human, people!

Thus, education must not be about an abstract universal or a shining theory but a particular life, a particular calling of a particular person with particular friends and relations and interests and attributes to share. This means an education true to the way we are as human persons must preserve the time and place and imagination required for us to know each other deeply, to listen, to respond, as humans are wired to do. It also means that if the "teachable moment" is the encounter with the Divine as Mason posits, the notebooks, with their implicit constraint for the particular of nuance, time and place, "fence the communion table" as it were, to preserve relationship and the hospitality of this encounter.[356]

~~~~~~~

This is not a prohibitive legalism however. Like any good liturgy, the notebooks free and protect the doctrine and the "holy of holies" of this profound hospitality. Perhaps Mason's *telos* can be approached with a negative example. Renowned philosophers, Jean Vanier and Stanley Hauerwas, argue in *Living Gently in a Violent World* that because as a culture we are losing our nuancefulness (or the celebration of beauty), as well as time-fulness and placefulness, we are losing our ability to be open to the other. Relationships require story, time, and stability. Quoting sad statistics on the incidence of abortion of Downs Syndrome children in France, Vanier and Hauwerwas warn of the profound inhospitality we are countenancing and the imminent danger of losing personhood in our idolatry of utility and efficiency.[357] "The reason that speed and placelessness are so important has everything to do with the current trust in technology and the mobility technology makes possible—indeed, makes necessary."[358] Seeing the communities Vanier began more than forty years ago for people living with disabilities, known as L'Arche, as a "sign and a sacrament," John Swinton, who writes the introduction and conclusion to this deep conversation between Vanier and Hauerwas, talks about the importance "of *embodying the paradigm shift* that allows us…to look differently at the world… Thus we discover the reality of a new time, a time for caring for those who do not promise to make the world a better place, a time for being with those who do not promise to contribute to our status."[359] Hauerwas and Vanier argue that peace or right relationships and community take time and create time, require placefulness, (stability and duration) and create it, require story and metaphor and also generate them.[360] Such hospitality is the requirement of the human flourishing with which Mason is inspired, the very bones and shape of life. And if L'Arche is called to be a sign and a sacrament against "utility," Mason posits no less; her life's work is to cause us to "realize something of the solemn and sacramental character of education, the outward and visible sign of that inward and spiritual grace—the life and growth of the human spirit."[361]

~ ~ ~ ~ ~ ~ ~

Thomas Armstrong, in his welcome volume *The Best Schools*, in many instances unknowingly points to the relational vision Mason is presenting. It is not surprising to those who know her that her method is bursting with "best practices." There is the obvious support for meditation and play Armstrong says children absolutely need.[362] There is her vital emphasis on imagination.[363] She relies on conversation through narration, notebooks, and the Grand Conversation, to work in concert with the child's natural oracy[364] and need for expression and belonging.[365] With Mason's practice, we model daily that sharing with a real person is not the same thing as visiting someone's webpage and ensure that education remains personal and relationship enhancing.[366] We dare to stay accountable through that classroom atmosphere and conversation to a rare shared understanding, to productive debate even; as you look at my notebook and I look at yours and we see that we are struck by the same material to express opposite points of view, we engage in the dialogue and cooperative learning we require.[367] Armstrong could not help but notice that Mason's array of notebooks makes an appeal for a sensory-rich and developmentally appropriate real-world education.[368]

As we ruminate over and choose the content and presentation for our notebook pages, we become assured of our own connected and intimate experience and trust rather less to the specialist, whom Mason asserts is "defunct."[369] By letting the blank page and the banquet lead us ever into that encounter that requires our participation and unique experience, our motivation is continually renewed; our decision-making is required.[370] Through our notebooks, we are interdisciplinary, and our learning is connected.[371] Through their emphasis on place, our learning is "community-based."[372]

And surely these are only some of the wonders preserved in Mason's notebook practice. As the Mason community gets stronger in these postures, no doubt new things will be revealed as fruitful and important. There are likely many surprising and hidden ways the forms of vitality support Mason's pedagogy and relationship. For instance, Armstrong notes that "rites of passage" are essential for adolescents and young adults, and one thinks of the value of new notebooks awaiting our students at different points in their school life—starting a new word book with the taking up of the second and maybe third language, moving from the first halting copybook to the Commonplace, scaffolding a growing self-awareness guided by *Ourselves* with a Map of Mansoul or a Fortitude Book.[373] There is the ever more complex timeline to create and the celebration of turning 10 and getting (finally) one's own Book of Centuries. According to Armstrong, these sorts of small celebrations are part of what makes a healthy atmosphere and a "best" school.[374]

We could go on with the list, but it is enough to notice how these paper graces ensure the knowledge is not abstract and stays oriented toward others and that the Living Page is a protection for "self-education" since it also protects the relationship of the teacher to her students. Without the notebooks, it would be too easy for the well-meaning teacher to lose track of "masterly inactivity," and the fact that "every effort made by the teacher to help in this process lessens the attention in the pupil."[375]

~~~~~~~

Esther De Waal, writer and scholar on St. Benedict's Rule, advises on "the dangers of popularizing and trivializing" writings from the past. She cautions that "to discover a tradition just because we need it can be a "dangerous undertaking," referring, I think, to our "so that" tendency.[376] In Mason, we find a 19th Century voice with so much to offer in our day. She seems to have thought of everything we are looking for in addressing the current educational challenges, yet there is a danger inherent in that very fact. If we have discovered a treasure, Mason will have us to acquire it only in the paradox of open-handedness. It reminds me of a very vivid story I requested over and over again when I was small. I can still picture the cave of treasure in my mind's eye (like Smaug's in Michael Hague's illustration of *The Hobbit*).

> According to legend, the leprechaun has a pot of gold hidden somewhere, and he must give up his treasure to the one who catches him. You'll have to step lively and think quickly to capture a leprechaun's gold, though, because this sly little fellow will fool you into looking away for an instant while he escapes into the forest.
> A story is told of the man who compelled a leprechaun to take him to the very bush where the gold was buried. The man tied a red handkerchief to the bush in order to

recognize the spot again and ran home for a spade. He was gone only three minutes, but when he returned to dig, there was a red handkerchief on every bush in the field.[377]

As soon as we try to grasp Mason's best practices for our remedy, we are in danger of losing them; we hear her whispering, "a utilitarian education is profoundly immoral."[378] Just like the leprechaun's gold, the Glory she implores us to keep sight of cannot be "kept" at all.

Keeping Glory

The forms of vitality invite us to this, then, the ultimate "resistant rear-ranging" of embodying this paradigm shift to hospitality, learning to "live with" children rather than to *do* education to them. Challenges facing us culturally and sociologically reveal a desperate need. Science is showing that Mason is reading the child aright, and it seems that the time is ripe to recover her quiet steps to a flourishing human society. But will we hear her on her own terms? We may know enough to realize her reemergence will be more than a quaint Victorian tea party, but will we be able to accept her as a visionary and a prophet recalling us to the "secret of knowing 'glory' when we see it?" Will we heed her call to keep returning to relationships? Will we be suspicious of technique and learn to gently support the connection that is ultimately without our power, through much talking about, drawing and writing in, and meditating over our notebooks? In a culture hell-bent on speed and efficiency, will we let Mason's notebooks grace us in reuniting body and spirit by the balance of books *and* things, propositions *and* artifacts, thinking *and* doing? Will we accept the invitation to confound the "invasion of materialism" and utility in these covert ways of being sign and symbol? [379]

~ ~ ~ ~ ~ ~ ~

De Waal considers the work of symbol with the help of author Flannery O'Connor:

> They (symbols) also hold layers of meaning, mysteries which reveal themselves—or are dug out—with time and attention. A symbol should 'go on deepening.' In this

telling phrase, Flannery O'Connor is reminding us that a symbol has the power not only to reveal the hitherto unknown, but also to call us forward and invite us to participate in something beyond itself.[380]

Beyond their simple pages can the forms of vitality do that—"go on deepening?" Can they humbly provide coherence and continuity for days that e-mail and social networks would chop up into "attention-diverting bits and pieces?"[381] Can they move us to honor the world's great, rare, and often sacred, artifacts by leading us to see a few of them for ourselves and draw each carefully, with awe, instead of reducing each to the common denominator of digital reproduction? Will we let the Commonplace slow our reading to Benedict's wisdom, whose monks received one book a year to read and chew on, digest, assimilate, and grow by? Welcoming this meditative notebook practice, will we do our own wee part in slowing this age's verbal, print, and visual onslaught? Mason says, "all important things are simple."[382] Will we take her at her word and be in touch with the great wisdom of the past to think through our own culture with these homely tools, a notebook and a pencil, rather than grab for the "pot of gold" of better student achievement?

De Waal relays a further analogy for symbol gleaned from Martin Smith, who sees, "the symbol as a token or counter like the stub of a theater ticket, which is not the performance itself but will take us to where the performance is."[383] I like that. Mason's paper postures are not the event in themselves, they continuously extend an invitation: Will you come to the Banquet?

~ ~ ~ ~ ~ ~ ~

And somehow, there is nothing greater than to witness the delivery and acceptance of this invitation. I had the privilege of observing such an "affair of the spirit"[384] when a lovely mother, quite new to Mason, discovered the Book of Firsts during a formation weekend. N. shared that her family was forced to leave their home in the Middle East for political reasons when she was a small child to emigrate to America. Somehow, while the Book of Firsts was for the rest of us in that session still a rather pedestrian concept, mildly sweet perhaps and a means of noticing seasonal changes, botany, etc., N. responded visibly to the exquisite invitation within it to Something

More. She shared with tears in her eyes the marvelous sense of community and "at tableness"[385] of the whispered, almost forgotten Middle Eastern practice of "sharing the first fruits." No one in her home country would ever think of picking the first tomato of the season for herself, she said. If persimmons were beginning to fruit, there would be a family celebration of them at the dinner table that night with everybody present. If the first rose of the year bloomed, it was given pride of place in a special vase in the living room, though thereafter roses might be picked with abandon and decorate any room in the house with liberality. In this simple but mindful way, the creation, Creator, and family were honored and brought together. Our sharing of this modest notebook practice, enlivened in a country so far from her own over a hundred years earlier, had brought this singular custom back to N. so vividly that all of us could hear the numinous summons to the kind of hospitality a Mason education at its best can foster.

In that moment, The Book of Firsts was not just pages and lines; it had become that "deepening" symbol—a living way to see beyond the facts to the Something More. N. happily recovered the ancient wisdom that we are not to be tinkered with like motorcycles under the care of a mechanic but are "educated by our intimacies."[386] And as the ancients knew who preserved that posture in N.'s home country, the possibility for that sacred encounter is all around us and may break out at any moment. With the eyes Mason ensures we have to see, such intimacies abound. Tucker Shaw, who observed his breakfast in his notebook every day for a whole year, found something wonderful in even that humble rhythm. Through his bowl of oatmeal, he says he became awake to the fact that "there is so much to consider." He said his notebook process became to him, "like saying grace!"[387]

~~~~~~

Can we keep Glory? No. "Who has solved for us the least of mysteries of birth and death and life?" Mason wisely asks.[388] But by having us assume their several expectant postures, our notebooks put us in what Marilynne Robinson calls "the way of the gift."[389] They become a doorway into the "Large Room." Foster calls this room "a richer attachment to God." Vanier and Hauerwas call it "Living Gently." Berry calls it "charity," and "Schultz "living virtuously."[390] We may not ever come to the end of defining Glory, but however we describe it, Mason is beckoning us into the fuller, deeper human life of mindfulness and attention. The Glory compels the gratitude of our records.[391] Like those under Benedict's Rule, the first word of which is "Listen," we learn under Mason's tutelage to wait, to watch, and to "hear keenly and sensitively that word of God which is not only message but event and encounter."[392]

Mason's students become thus "students of Divinity" and the Living Page a protection for these almost hidden postures leading to Wisdom. Keepers assume fidelity to the particular to preserve personhood through Nuance, Time, Place, and Relationships. They enter that Large Room where care about their planet, their homes, their government, and each other becomes possible. As Berry says, we must keep deeply the parable of the lost sheep; Divinity seeks the one and leaves the others. Love is particular; the abstract is a sin, as inattention is a sin.[393] Each encounter with our notebook utters the conviction, "there are no Great Thinkers; there is only Van Gogh, Plutarch, Churchill, Shakespeare, and Aristotle." "The Environment cannot be loved, but Vroman's Nose and Rufner Mountain, Point Pelee, and Lake Nipissing can." If we are going to "know Glory" we are going to have to be specific and have a relationship to that particular burning bush with our particular feet and without our particular shoes.

~ ~ ~ ~ ~ ~ ~

In this paradigm-shifted way of life—along the way to "becoming truth," to quote Foster again, our notebooks are companions. One of New's interviewees says the notebooks are "omnipresent, they live life with (us.)"[394] To keep them is like walking with Mason herself and hearing her keep pace, no matter what your spiritual convictions, with the old, old prayer, attributed to Saint Irenaeus, "The glory of God is a human being fully alive; and to be alive consists in beholding God."[395] Mason will have us push back "the causes of deadness to things divine" and join a cosmic game of freeze tag.[396] We develop the mien of hospitality that will conserve or invite the awakening in others. It can begin as simply as considering a medium consistent with our message. If we give children a hodgepodge of papers, bought at 35 cents per 100, cleared out at the end of the term till the trashcans are overflowing, what are we really saying? "Your work is dispensable, not important?" "Someday you will grow up. Then, you will do real work; you will have permanent notes, important things like files and journals and freedom to choose what goes into them." By then, God forbid, the students may no longer be awake.

~ ~ ~ ~ ~ ~ ~

In my heart's eye, is an enchanting, "naturally caffeinated" boy of nine, beleaguered, shirt tail out, smears of pencil lead and playground on his inquisitive face, eyes trying so hard to discern what is wanted in the foreign ground of the classroom. We know the story too well; in his frustration and confinement, Glory is becoming more and more a miasma obscured by the rules and the sitting and the holes rubbed straight through bizarre assignments with erasers obviously meant more for filling peashooters than correcting papers. His is a classroom the same as so many others that will unpin imagination from the soul, and drain yet another day of mystery and beauty. We know it, but how many times will another term be wiped up and swept into the bin whilst the real schooling of the all too short summer pours in at the windows?

Can we abandon the smell of egg salad sandwiches and gym clothes of our constraints for rustling slopes and chirping frogs? What will finally make us free enough to value hay sticking in shreds to the sweat of the back and books (real ones) savored on damp grass in spruce forts while cicadas whirr and the school gates and asphalt fade far away in more than just the summer's heat? GLORY. Write it down. Don't lose track of it; keep it close to your heart.

The Living Page is a returning to the incarnational. It is a return to the primeval garden, alive with that ancient knowing. The prophet tells us that people have changed their glory for that which does not profit," (Jer, 2:11) but there is a universal invitation to return as Hinchman celebrates:

> Each of us is supplied with the same basic equipment as the first human, and lives under the conditions that make being human so remarkable; we have an arsenal of sense, in a world of count-less things to sense. We have minds that can hold images and form ideas of past, present, and future all at once. We have won a moment in the unfolding universe. Doesn't that warrant com-ment?[397]

Mason tells her student teachers, "In a sense each of us is a voice, we all seek expression; the more modes of expression we find, the fuller and richer is our life. Expression is to us life; suppression death."[398] The rocks themselves will cry out. There can be no greater apologetic for the Living

Page. We are told there were, at Scale How, Mason's House of Education, "no methods courses."[399] Cholmondley writes that the House of Education was "an unwalled university of plain living and high thinking."[400] It was "all living." The two years of teacher training consisted simply of the feast and the practice because Mason sees, like Hauerwas and Vanier, "a vital aspect of a paradigm shift is the need for exemplars—people or groups who can model the new paradigm, challenge our presuppositions and draw us into the belief that the new paradigm might actually be possible." If we want the full life she was seeing, we can do no less (or more!)[401]

Ultimately, the Living Page offers us a posture of humility. On the one hand, the way we use our paper can seem too small and simple a thing to make a difference. And, what will our parents think or our colleagues? On the other hand, to live this can seem too lofty an invitation. Each notebook with its own guiding principles and purpose can even seem an encumbrance, intimidating. We do not know where to begin; who can feel herself up to the task of living out the paradigm shift?

Mason knows what is in us. "Seeing there are so many things we cannot know, our need for humility is great."[402] It is also a comfort to read what Hauerwas said of L'Arche: it "is a modest proposal. You've got to begin somewhere." [403] Through our relationships with children, we see our work, our *opus dei*, and understand it must be an offering. Our practice need not be perfect to begin to ripen us into people who see beyond what is to what ought to be, and who believe that in taking up these few postures of sustained attention we can and will be open to the mysterious transformation.

Mason wisely encourages her fledgling teachers, "it is so good to think that any good work we carry on will be carried on."[404] She refuses to take herself too seriously. If she knows what is in us, she also knows how little lies with us; these true principles worked out in simple, quotidian ceremonies of Keeping *will* assert themselves, as a babe takes to the breast: "men *must* not only attend and receive spiritual food, but they *must* assimilate it with some process, answering to what we call digestion in the case of physical food; they *must* meditate upon what they have heard, ponder in their hearts, '*keep it*,' live upon it."[405] May her view of Glory continue to cause us "to study in many ways the art of standing aside" and make Keepers of us all.

Appendix A. Keeping Supplies

In the Scriptorium:

I resurrect the term Scriptorium in deference to the monasteries of the Dark Ages that steadfastly dedicated themselves to preserving manuscripts and illuminating texts for the coming generations in hopes that our "keeping" of these forms of vitality may play some small part in the drama of our day. It is my fond hope that whatever we call them, we will create dedicated spaces for writing, drawing, and thinking worthy of these important practices and conducive to inspiration and our most careful work.

Across a Dark and Wild Sea by Don Brown is a lovely picture book about such a monk, Columcille. Brown writes, "Reading and writing were like magic, and the people who knew their secrets as rare as wizards." There are myriad ways to set up a space for Keeping, and I have no particular prescription beyond Mason's dependence on simplicity and beauty. But it seems to me this quote of Brown's projects the right atmosphere. Reading and writing are like magic, and we want to do everything in our power to make sure the people who know this are not at all rare. While all that is really needed is a notebook and a pen and pencil, here are some ideas for what to include as funds or occasion suggest.

Flower presses

Various glues and adhesives

Paper cutter

Fine-tipped black pens

Various straight edges, rulers

Watercolor pencils (Prism is a good brand)

Pencils (regular, primary and sketching)

Sharpeners

Erasers

Dictionaries in several languages, thesaurus

Artist's or drafting table

Solid, appropriately sized writing tables

Computer/printer for reference, typeface, recording narrations, etc.

Selection of books on keeping notebooks, how-to drawing books, book making/binding

Sample student pages

Posters of beautiful scripts graphic designs, borders

Shelves for housing notebooks, bins, baskets for class set

Wool, magnet, foam, & wooden letters for letter play, sand tray for making letters

All kinds of inviting notebooks and papers: lined, graph papers of various sized squares, tracing paper, watercolor paper, sketch papers, cardstock, scrap paper, cardboard, newsprint, brown Kraft paper, etc.

Date stamp and ink

Scissors

Paintbrushes

Watercolor boxes

Displays for collections and student work

Dry-erase, chalkboards

Chart paper/stands, easels

Staplers, twine, tapes, and other binding materials

Punches, three-hole, single

Paper trays, caddies, cans, baskets to organize supplies

Large clips for holding paper, books open

Comfortable chairs/ cozy carpets, cushions for sitting

Appropriate task lighting, preferably lots of daylight

In the field:

A daily walk with the chance to narrate what one has seen is all that is essential but a travel bag (perhaps sewn as a handicraft) could contain some of the following:

An all-tool or jackknife (scissors, pliers, blade, screwdriver, etc.)

Hand lens or magnifying glass

Nature notebook

Travel watercolors

Pencil

Tweezers

Collection containers: jars, bags, small tins, film containers, matchboxes

Tape/glue stick

Camera and/or recording device

Binoculars

Gloves

Appendix B. Notebook Samples

Book of Firsts (*photo Laurie Bestvater*)

10/21/03

There are many times when you cannot help but
there is no time when you cannot give help. —

George Merriam.

Oct 28, '03

"Be of good comfort, master Ridley,
and play the man," said Latimer, as they
were being led to be burned together,
"we shall this day light such a candle,
by God's grace, in England, as I trust
shall never be put out."

Copybook Form I *(photo Laurie Bestvater)*

Oct 11, 07

"The answer was a harsh gabbling which they all felt immediately to be exotic. Wherever the Bird came from, it was obviously somewhere far away. The accent was strange and guttural, the speech distorted. They could catch only a word here and there.

'Come beel - Rah! Rah! - you beel-yark-tink me finish me no finish-'urt you dam' The dark brown head flickered from side to side. Then unexpectedly it began to drive it's beak into the ground. They noticed for the first time that grass in front of it was torn and scored with lines. For some moments it stabbed here and there; then gave up, lifted its head and watched them again."

<u>Watership Down</u> ch. 23

Copybook Form III *(photo Laurie Bestvater)*

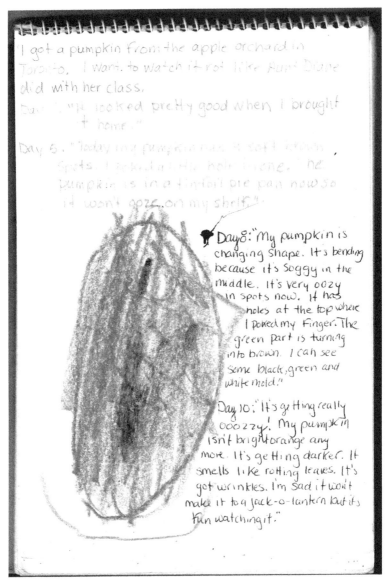

I got a pumpkin from the apple orchard in
Toronto. I want to watch it rot like Aunt Diane
did with her class.

Day [...] "It looked pretty good when I brought
        it home."

Day 6. "Today my pumpkin has 4 soft brown
        spots. I poked at the soft brown. The
        pumpkin is in a tinfoil pie pan now so
        it won't ooze on my shelf."

Day 8: "My pumpkin is
changing shape. It's bending
because it's soggy in the
middle. It's very oozy
in spots now. It has
holes at the top where
I poked my finger. The
green part is turning
into brown. I can see
some black, green and
white mold."

Day 10: "It's getting really
ooozzy. My pumpkin
isn't bright orange any
more. It's getting darker. It
smells like rotting leaves. It's
got wrinkles. I'm sad it won't
make it to a jack-o-lantern but it's
fun watching it."

Nature Notebook Form I *(photo Laurie Bestvater)*

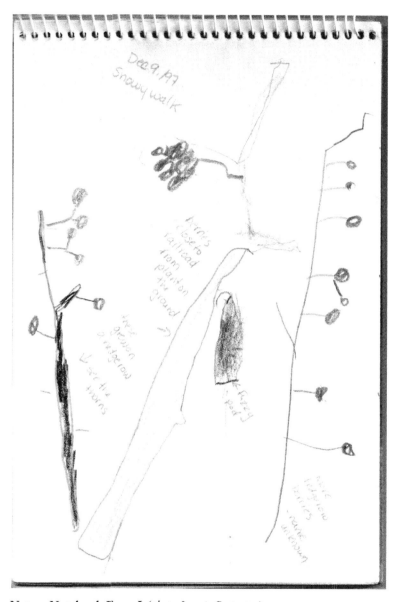

Nature Notebook Form I *(photo Laurie Bestvater)*

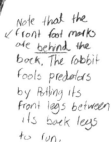

Note that the
← front foot marks
are behind the
back. The rabbit
fools predators
by putting its
front legs between
its back legs
to run.

wild rabbit

NatureNotebook Form III *(photo Laurie Bestvater)*

American Robin
April 20, 2006
the Robins will
come back early
in the spring but
won't start singing
until he or she has
a mate.

May 18th, 2006

patula
sail.
il saw this
guy in Switz
erland.

Nature Notebook Form III *(photo Laurie Bestvater)*

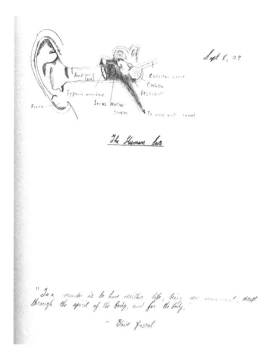

Nature Notebook Form IV *(photo photo Laurie Bestvater)*

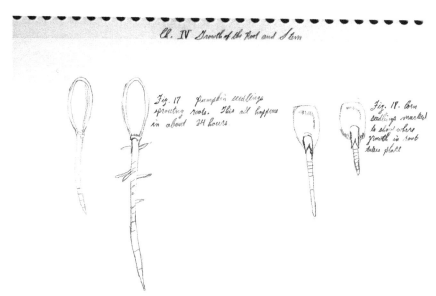

Nature Notebook Form V *(photo Laurie Bestvater)*

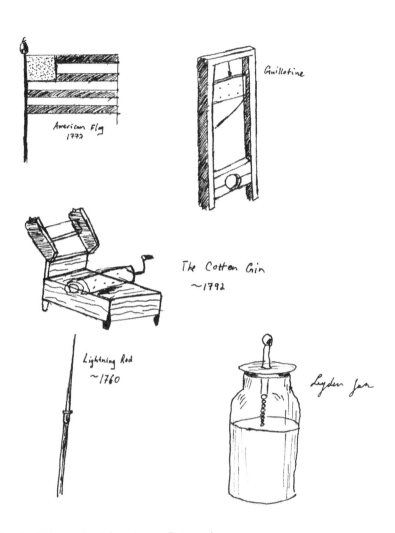

Labels within image: *Guillotine*; *American Flag 1772*; *The Cotton Gin ~1792*; *Lightning Rod ~1760*; *Leyden Jar*

Book of Centuries *(photo Laurie Bestvater)*

18th Century CE

	5
	10
	15
	20
	25
	30
	35
	40
	45
	50
	55
Mozart b.	60
	65
	Beethoven b. 70
	Am. Revolution b. 75
Haydn B.	80
Articles of Confederation	85
Am. Constitution	*Fr. Revolution b.* 90
	95
	100

Book of Centuries *(photo Laurie Bestvater)*

Appendix C. Way of the Will Chart

A king is not a king unless he reigns and a man is less than a man unless he wills."

– Mason, *Philosophy*, 133

Wilful	**Governed by Will**
Led by "I want," desires, habit, convention, appetite, influenced, drifting, impulsive, passion, weakens will,	*Choosing, deciding, conscious, definite, self-directed, "Premier of Mansoul," aims beyond self, constant, strengthens character*

Unworthy or Evil ends	Worthy or Good ends	Unworthy or Evil ends	Worthy or Good ends

Steps to willing: (Mason, 135)
1. An idea is presented.
2. We accept the notion and ponder on it.
3. We vaguely intend to act upon it.
4. We form a definite purpose or resolution.
5. A definite act or general temper of mind follows.

Appendix D. General Charlotte Mason Lesson Plan

Subject:

Class: Age: Time:

Objectives/ ideas:

Books and Things:

Location & preparation:

Lesson:

Step. 1. Introduce lesson with interest and background information

Step 2. Narrate last day's portion briefly

Step 3. Read and narrate or use/examine real thing and narrate

Step 4. Grand Conversation and questions

Step 5. Notebooks if applicable*

Appendix E. Sources

Best Containers http://www.bestcontainers.com
boxes, jars, and tins for collections.

Books of Centuries http://www.BookofCenturies.com
Constructed after Bernau's design.

Book Factory http://www.bookfactory.com
Custom Lab books.

Book of Firsts http://redmountaincommunityschool.com
Created by Red Mountain Community School.

Dick Blick http://www.dickblick.com
Notebooks, including Moleskine, & art supplies.

Field Notes http://fieldnotesbrand.com/shop/
Notebooks for agricultural or geographic work.

Hollanders http://www.hollanders.com
Papers, Bookbinding Supplies & Workshops.

Kate's Paperie http://www.katespaperie.com
Notebooks, beautiful stationery.

Mercurius http://www.mercurius-usa.com
Notebooks and natural art supplies.

Nature's Pressed Flowers http://www.naturespressed.com
Flower presses, tools and materials for collecting.

New York Public Library Digital Gallery http://digitalgallery.nypl.org
Images for Book of Centuries.

Paper Presentation http://www.paperpresentation.com
Papers, folders, tags & labels.

Paper Source http://www.papersource.com
Beautiful papers and art supplies

Tree Cycle http://www.treecycle.com
Recycled stationery.

Bibliography

Anderson, Eve. *Book of Centuries.* [unpublished artifact]. Charlotte Mason Digital Collection. Redeemer University College. http://charlottemason.redeemer.ca/PNEU-Briefcase/PNEU-Box24/pneu162/i3p01p42pneu162.pdf.

Andreloa, Karen, ed. [untitled article] reprinted in *The Parents' Review 1* (Winter, 1992): 14.

"Ansel Adams," *Think Exist.* http://thinkexist.com/quotation/notebook_no_photographer_should_be_without_one/223012.html (accessed May, 2012).

Armstrong, Thomas. *The Best Schools.* Alexandria, VA: Association for Supervision and Curriculum Development, 2006.

B. H. "History: Teaching Practically Considered." *The Parents' Review*, IV, (1893/4): 890-896. Ambleside Online. http://www.amblesideonline.org/PR/PR04p890History.shtml.

Baden Powell, Lord. "Be Prepared," *The Listener.* (1937) The Pine Tree Web. http://www.pinetreeweb.com/bp-listener.htm.

Barbery, Muriel. *The Elegance of the Hedgehog.* Translated by Alison Anderson. New York: Europa Editions. 2008.

Beale, Dorothea. "The Teaching of Chronology," *The Parents' Review*, 2 (2) 1891: 81-90, Ambleside Online. http://www.amblesideonline.org/PR/PR02p081Chronology.shtml.

Bernau, G.M. "The Book of Centuries." *Parents' Review* (34) 1923: 720-724, Ambleside Online. http://www.amblesideonline.org/PR/PR34p720BookofCenturies.shtm.

--- "*The Book of Centuries and How to Keep One.*" London: Parents' National Education Union, n.d. Charlotte Mason Digital Collection. Redeemer University College. http://charlottemason.redeemer.ca/2nd-CM-Briefcase/Box16/cmc107/I/i1p01-p15cmc107I.pdf.

--- "Century Books." *Parents' Union School's Diamond Jubilee Magazine*, (1951): 42-44. Charlotte Mason Digital Collection. Redeemer University College. http://charlottemason.redeemer.ca/2nd-CM-Briefcase/Box17/cmc113/p001-p070cmc113.pdf.

Bernier, Benjamin. post to Charlotte Mason Series discussion list, "CM Series, 03 Notes on the Heart," January 4, 2013, http://groups.yahoo.com/group/CMSeries/message/14364.

Berry, Wendell. *The Art of the Commonplace: the Agrarian Essays of Wendell Berry.* Edited by Norman Wirzba. Washington: Shoemaker & Hoard, 2002.

--- *Jayber Crow.* New York: Counterpoint Press, 2000.

Bestvater, Laurie. "Notes on the Fear of Bathmats," *Charlotte Mason Educational Review* 3(1) 2008: 38-43. ChildlightUSA. http://www.child-lightusa.org/review/Spring2008_Review.pdf.

--- "Book of Centuries Revisited," *ChildlightUSA.* http://childlightusa.wordpress.com/2010/08/15the-book-of-centuries-revisited-by-laurie-best-vater/.

--- "Book of Centuries Revisited—Part II" *ChildlightUSA.* http://child-lightusa.wordpress.com/2011/03/28/the-book-of-centuries-revisited-part-ii-by-laurie-bestvater/.

"Bookbinding," *Wikipedia,* http://en.wikipedia.org/wiki/Bookbinding (accessed August 23, 2012).

Brookes, Mona. *Drawing with Children.* Tenth Anniversary ed. Berkley, CA: Putnam Books. 1995.

Brown, Don. *Across a Dark and Wild Sea.* New York: Roaring Brook Press, 2002.

Caine, R. N., Caine, G., McClintic, C. L., and Klimek, K. J. ed.s *12 Brain/Mind Learning Principles in Action: Developing Executive Functions of the Human Brain.* 2nd ed. Thousand Oaks, CA: Sage Publishing, 2008.

Campbell, B. & Foulton, L. *Science Notebooks: Writing about Inquiry.* Portsmouth *NH:* Heinnemann, 2003.

"Student Centered Notebooks," *Science and Children* (Nov./Dec. 2004): 26-29. National Science Teachers Association. http://www.esiponline.org/csl/presentations/lorifulton.pdf.

Capehart, Wendi, *"Learning Styles and Graphic Media: Should Pictures Have a Place in Education?"* Ambleside Online. http://www.amblesideonline.org/BooksPicturesshtml.

Carr, Nicholas, "Is Google Making us Stupid?" *The Atlantic,* July/August (2008) http://www.theatlantic.com/doc/200807/google.

Cholmondley, Essex. *The Story of Charlotte Mason.* Reprint 1960. Petersfield, Hants, Great Britain: Child Light Ltd. 2000.

Clark, J. H. *"Chatelaine & Aide Memoir,"* Morning Glory Jewelry. http://www.morninggloryjewelry.com/chatelaine-aide-memoire-aid-63.html.

Coombs, Margaret,. "One Comment," [online forum comment]. http://childlightusa.wordpress.com/2012/09/09/why-homeschool-a-la-charlotte-mason-by-mary-c-gildersleeve/ (accessed Sept. 13, 2012).

"Commonplace Books," *Wikipedia,* http://en.wikipedia.org/wiki/Commonplace_book (accessed 2011).

Crawford, Matthew. B. *Shop Class as Soulcraft: An Inquiry into the Value of Work.* New York: Penguin Press, 2009.

De Waal, Esther. *Seeking God: The Way of St. Benedict.* Collegeville, Minnesota: Liturgical Press, 2001.

--- *Seeking life: The Baptismal Invitation of the Rule of St. Benedict.* Collegeville, Minnesota: Liturgical Press, 2001.

Deck, M. *Nature Notebook*. [unpublished artifact]. Charlotte Mason Digital Collection. Redeemer University College. http://charlottemason.redeemer.ca/2ndCMBriefcase/ALMBox127cmc519/i1p083p158cmc519.pdf.

Deedy, Carmen Agra, illustrated by Laura L. Seely. *Agatha's Featherbed*. Atlanta: Peachtree Pub Ltd., 1994.

Didion, Joan. *Slouching towards Bethlehem*. New York: Farrar, Straus & Giroux, 1966.

Egan, Kieran. *Children's Minds, Talking Rabbits & Clockwork Oranges*. Columbia University, New York: Teachers College Press, 1999.

Engle, M. *Summer Birds: The butterflies of Maria Merian*. New York: Henry Holt & Company, 2010.

"Enquire Within Upon Everything," *Wikipedia,* http://en.wikipedia.org/wiki/Enquire_Within_Upon_Everything (accessed 2011).

Foster, Richard. *Celebration of Discipline*. 25th Anniversary ed. San Francisco: Harper, 1998.

---. "Made Visible and Plain: On Spiritual Writing.," *A Syllable of Water.* Edited by E. Griffin, Brewster, MA: Paraclete Press, 2008.

Frankl, Victor, E. *Man's Search for Meaning*. New York: Pocket Books, 1963.

Fredrickson, B. "Your Phone vs. Your Heart," *Sunday Review*, New York Times, March, 23, 2013, http://www.nytimes.com/2013/03/24/opinion/sunday/your-phone-vs-your-heart.html?_r=1&.

Fujimura, Mako. *Refractions*. Colorado Springs, CO: Navpress, 2009.

Gaillet, Lynee. "Commonplace Books and the Teaching of Style," *Journal of Teaching Writing*, Vol.15 (2)(2010): 285-294. http://journals.iupui.edu/index.php/teachingwriting/article/viewFile/1208/1169.

"Gilbert White," *Wikipedia,* http://en.wikipedia.org/wiki/Gilbert_White (accessed 2011).

"George Washington's School Copybook," *Reason: American Treasures of the Library of Congress.* http://www.loc.gov/exhibits/treasures/trr048.html.

"Georgia O'Keef*e*," *Brainy Quotes,* http://www.brainyquote.com/quotes/quotes/g/georgiaok134583.html (accessed December 23, 2011).

"The Glory of God is Man Fully Alive." *Ten Thousand Places,* http://tenthousandplaces.org/2009/04/25/the-glory- of-god-is-man-fully-alive/.

"The Gods of the Copywork Headings." *Wikipedia,* http://en.wikipedia.org/wiki/The_Gods_of_the_Copybook_Headings (accessed June 21, 2012).

Godden, Rumer. *China Court: The Hours of a Country House.* New York: William Morrow and Company, Inc., 1960/61.

Government of Ontario, "Grand Conversations in Primary Classrooms," *Capacity Building Series,* Secretariat Special Edition: no.18 (April, 2011): 1-8. http://www.edu.gov.on.ca/eng/literacynumeracy/inspire/research/cbs_grand_conversations.pdf

Graham, Abbie. *Ceremonials of Common Days.* New York: The Woman's Press, 1923.

Gregory, Danny. *An Illustrated Life: Drawing Inspiration from the Private Sketchbooks of Artists, Illustrators and Designers.* Cincinnati: How Books, 2008.

Griffin, E., ed. *A Syllable of Water.* Brewster, Mass: Paraclete Press, 2009.

Gudgel, Andrew. "Commonplace books -- Old Wine in New Bottles." *Andrew Gudgel's Writing Blog,* http://www.andrewgudgel.com/commonplace.htm.

Guroian, Vigen. "Awakening the Moral Imagination: Teaching virtues through Fairy Tales." *The Intercollegiate Review* Fall (1996): 3-13.

Guroian, Vigen. *Tending the Heart of Virtue: How Classic Stories Awaken a Child's Moral Imagination.* London: Oxford University Press, 1998.

Harvard University Library, "Commonplace Books." *Reading: Harvard Views of Readers, Readership and Reading History.* http://ocp.hul.harvard.edu/reading/commonplace.html.

Hauerwas, Stanley and Jean Vanier, *Living Gently in a Violent World: The Prophetic Witness of Weakness.* Downer's Grove, IL: InterVarsity Press Books, 2008.

Hinchman, Hannah. *A Life in Hand: Creating the Illuminated Journal.* Salt Lake City: Peregrine Smith Books, 1991.

Hinchman, Hannah. *A Trail through the Leaves.* New York: W. W. Norton & Company, 1999.

Household, H.W. *P.N.E.U. Methods of Teaching: with Special Reference to the Teaching of English.* [eight-page pamphlet]. Charlotte Mason Digital Collection. Redeemer University College.http://charlottemason.redeemer. ca/2nd-CM-Briefcase/Box16/cmc107/II/i1p1-i2p3cmc107II.pdf.

Houston, James. *Joyful Exiles: Life on the Dangerous Edge of Things.* Downers Grove, IL: Intervarsity Press, 2006.

"How to Recycle Office Paper into Blank Books." *Instructables,* http:// www.instructables.com/id/How-to-recycle-office-paper-into-blank-books/?ALLSTEPS (accessed June 20, 2012).

Hugman, K. *House of Education Natural History Notebook.* 1922. [unpublished artifact]. Charlotte Mason Digital Collection. Redeemer University College. http://charlottemason.redeemer.ca/Box22/cmc147/ i1p01-p92cmc147.pdf.

"The Legend of the Leprechaun," *Irish Blessings.* http://www.irishindeed. com/page.htm?pg=LEPRECHAUN%20MYTH.

Irving, Winifred. *Notes on Making a Time-line.* [undated pamphlet]. London: Parents' National Educational Union. Charlotte Mason Digital Collection. Redeemer University College. http://charlottemason. redeemer.ca/2nd-CM-Briefcase/Box16/cmc107/I/i3p1-p4cmc107I.pdf.

"John Muir Journals." *Holt-Atherton Special Collections.* University of the Pacific. http://www.pacific.edu/Library/Find/Holt-Atherton-Special-Collections/John-Muir-Papers.html.

King, H. (2011). "Alexander Technique Teacher in North London." *Hillary King,* http://www.hilaryking.net/.

Kitching, Elsie. "Concerning Repeated Narration." *The Parent's Review*, 31(1)(1928): 58-62. Ambleside Online. http://www.amblesideonline.org/PR/PR39p058RepeatedNarration.shtml.

Klentschy, M. *Using Science Notebooks in Elementary Classrooms*. USA: National Science Teachers Association Press, 2008.

Klug, Ron. *How to Keep a Spiritual Journal: A Guide to Journal Keeping for Inner Growth and Personal Discovery*. Revised ed. Minneapolis: Augsburg Fortress, 2002.

Koker, M., D. Duquin, D. & K. Burke. "Frequently asked Questions about Science Notebooks." *Center for Educational Innovation Public Education Association*, https://sites.google.com/site/ceipeascience/research-on-science-notebooking (accessed 2010).

Lassner, Phyllis, and Lucy Le-Guilcher. ed.s *Rumer Godden: International and Intermodern Storyteller*. Burlington, VT: Ashgate Publishing. 2010.

"Lectio divina." *Wikipedia*, http://en.wikipedia.org/wiki/Lectio_Divina (accessed January 13, 2013).

Leslie, Clare Walker, and Chuck. E. Roth, *Keeping a Nature Journal*. 2nd ed. North Adams, MA: Storey Publishing. 2003.

Leslie, Clare Walker. *The Nature Connection: An Outdoor Workbook*. North Adams, MA.: Storey Publishing, 2010.

Lewin-Benham, Ann. *Infants & Toddlers at Work: Using Reggio-inspired Materials to Support Brain Development*. New York: Teachers College Press, 2010.

Lewis, Clive Staples. *Mere Christianity*. London: Fontana. 1963.

"Linus Pauling." *Wikipedia*, http://en.wikipedia.org/wiki/Linus_Pauling (accessed Sept. 11, 2012).

"Linus Pauling Research Notebooks." *Special Collections Oregon State University*.http://osulibrary.oregonstate.edu/specialcollections/rnb/.

Macbeth, S. *Praying in Color for Kids*. Brewster MA: Paraclete Press. 2009.

MacKay, Bret, and Kate Mackay. "The Manly Tradition of the Pocket Notebook." *The Art of Manliness,* http://artofmanliness.com/2010/08/23/the-manly-tradition-of-the-pocket-notebook/.

Margolis, K., and S. Trimble. "Paying Attention: An Interview with Barry Lopez." *Orion,* Summer (1990) Envirolink. http://arts.envirolink.org/interviews_and_conversations/BarryLopez.html.

"Marshall McLuhan," *Wikipedia,* http://en.wikipedia.org/wiki/Marshall_McLuhan (accessed October 22, 2012).

Mason, Charlotte Maria Shaw. *Formation of Character.* reprint 1905. Wheaton, IL: Tyndale House Publishers Inc., 1989.

---. *Home education.* reprint 1896. Wheaton, IL: Tyndale House Publishers, Inc., 1989.

---. *Ourselves.* reprint 1904. Wheaton, IL: Tyndale House Publishers Inc., 1989.

---. *Parents and Children.* reprint 1896. Wheaton, IL: Tyndale House Publishers Inc., 1989.

---. *A Philosophy of Education.* reprint 1925. Wheaton IL: Tyndale House Publishers Inc., 1989.

---. *The Reading Habit and a Wide Curriculum: The Curriculum of the Child is the Provision for the Man.* [Talk prepared for unknown presentation] Charlotte Mason Digital Collection. Redeemer University College. http://charlottemason.redeemer.ca/PNEU-Briefcase/PNEU-Box04/pneu49/i04p01-p25pneu49.pdf.

---. *Scale How Meditations.* Edited by Benjamin Bernier. LuLu, 2011.

---. *School education.* reprint 1904. Wheaton, IL: Tyndale House Publishers Inc., 1989.

McGonigal, Kelly. *The Willpower Instinct: How Self-control Works, Why it Matters and What you Can do to Get More of It.* New York: Avery, 2012.

In Memoriam, London: Parents National Education Union, 1923. Ambleside Online. http://www.amblesideonline.org/CM/InMemoriamIV.html.

Metroland News Service, "Bruce Cockburn Thanks McMaster for 'accepting all my crap.'" *Metro,* May 8, 2013, http://metronews.ca/news/hamilton/664074/bruce-cockburn-thanks-mcmaster-for-accepting-all-my-crap/.

Metzger, Mike. "The Wrong Winner," *Doggie Head Tilt,* http://www.doggieheadtilt.com/the-wrongwinner/.

Metzger, Mike. "More Lyrics," *Doggie Head Tilt,* http://www.doggieheadtilt.com/more-lyrics/#more-1141.

Moulton, G. E. "The Missing Journals of Merriweather Lewis," *Journals of the Lewis and Clarke Expedition.* University of Nebraska Lincoln. http://lewisandclarkjournals.unl.edu/read/?_xmlsrc=lc.missing.

Neiwert, Rachel A. "Savages or Citizens? Children, Education, and the British Empire, 1899-1950." PhD diss., University of Minnesotta, 2009. Proquest, Umi Dissertation Publishing. http://www.uread.com/book/savages-or-citizens-children-education/9781244071513.

Nesbitt, D.M.H. "The Teaching of History." *The Parents' Review.* (1901): 917-929. Ambleside Online. http://www.amblesideonline.org/PR/PR12p917TeachingofHistory.shtml.

New, Jennifer. *Drawing from Life: The Journal as Art.* New York: Princeton Architectural Press, 2005.

Ney, Marian W. *Charlotte Mason: A Pioneer of Sane Education.* Nottingham, GB: Educational Heretics Press, 1997.

O'Ferrell. Miss. "The Work and Aims of the Parents' Union School." *Parents' Review*, 33(11)(1922): 777-787. Ambleside Online. http://www.amblesideonline.org/PR/PR33p777WorkAimsofPUS.shtml.

"Paul Coelho," *Brainy Quotes*, http://www.brainyquote.com/quotes/authors/p/paulo_coelho.htm (accessed December 23, 2011).

Parents' National Education Union. *Exam 94 IV 1922.* Ambleside Online. http://www.amblesideonline.org/Exam94IV.shtml.

Parents' National Education Union. *School Programme 1896*. Ambleside Online. http://www.amblesideonline.org/Programme01I.shtml .

Parents' National Education Union. *Specimen Programme of a Term's Work 1921*. Ambleside Online. http://www.amblesideonline.org/FormI.shtml .

Parents' National Education Union. (1922). *School Programme 1922*. Ambleside Online. http://www.amblesideonline.org/Programme94VI.shtml.

Parents' National Education Union. *School Programme 1924*. London: Ambleside Online. http://www.charlottemason.redeemer.ca/2nd-CM-Briefcase/Box14/cmc96/:2Ap1-i4Bp6cmc96.Pdf .

Partnoy, Frank. *Wait: The Art and Science of Delay*. New York: Public Affairs Press, 2012.

PBS. "Tesla Master of Lightning." PBS. http://www.pbs.org/tesla/ll/index.html .

Pearcey, Nancy. *Saving Leonardo: A Call to Resist the Secular Assault on Mind, Morals & Meaning*. B & N Publishing Group, 2010.

Perlingieri, I. S. "Paintresses: Victorian Women China Painters and Potters." *New England Antiques Journal*, (2007). http://www.antiquesjournal.com/Pages04/Monthly_pages/march07/paintresses.html.

Pennethorne, R. A. "P.N.E.U Principles as Illustrated by Teaching." *The Parents 'Review*, 8, (1897): 549. http://www.amblesideonline.org/PR/PR10p549PNEUPrinciplesIllustrated.shtml.

Postman, Neil. *Amusing Ourselves to Death*. New York: Penguin. 1985.

Postman, Neil. *Technopoly*. New York: Alfred A. Knopf, 1992.

Rees, Brenda. "Student-driven Sense-making Notebooks." *What's the Big Idea*, 9(5) (2010): 1-4. K-12 Alliance. http://k12alliance.org/newsletters/WTBI-1005.pdf.

Reppman, M. "A Few words about the P.N.E.U.," *The Parents' Review*, vol. 12 (1901): 701-710. Ambleside Online. http://www.amblesideonline.org/PR/PR12p701PNEU.shtml.

Robinson, Sir Ken. "Imagination and Empathy," (Performer) (2011, Nov. 21). *Educating the Heart*. The Delailama Center, http://www.youtube.com/watch?v=Yu2zcmb3yAQ.

Robinson, Marilynne. *When I was a Child I read Books*. New York: Farrar, Straus and Giroux, 2012.

Rutgers University. "*Thomas Edison and his Papers*." Rutgers University. http://edison.rutgers.edu/papers.htm.

Schaeffer, Francis. A. *True Spirituality*. 30th anniversary ed. Wheaton, IL: Tyndale House Publishers, 2001.

Schultze, Quentin, J. *Habits of the High-tech Heart: Living Virtuously in the Information Age*. Grand Rapids, MI: Baker Publishing, 2002.

Scott, R. (2009, Aug. 6). "Galileo's Notebooks May Reveal Secrets of New Planet." *Uninews*. University of Melbourne. http://archive.uninews.unimelb.edu.au/view-43922.html.

Seerveld, Calvin G. *Rainbows for the Fallen World*, Toronto: Tuppence Press, 2005.

Smith, E. E. "There's More to Life than Being Happy." *The Atlantic*, Jan. 9, 2013. http://www.theatlantic.com/health/archive/2013/01/theres-more-to-life-than-being-happy/266805/.

Smith, E. K. *How to Make Books*. New York: Potter Craft, 2007.

Smith, J. Carroll. "Introducing Charlotte Mason's Use of Narration." *Forum on Public Policy*, Summer (2008): 1-13. http://forumonpublicpolicy.com/summer08papers/archivesummer08/smith.carroll.pdf.

Smith, James K.A. *Desiring the Kingdom: Worship, Worldview and Cultural Formation*. Grand Rapids: Baker Academic, 2009.

Smith, K. *How to be an Explorer of the World: Portable art Life Museum*. New York: A Perigee Book, 2008.

Stonehouse, Catherine, and Scottie May. *Listening to Children on the Spiritual Journey*. Grand Rapids, MI: Baker Publishing, 2010.

University of Virginia, "I Rise with the Sun." *Thomas Jefferson Foundation.* University of Virginia. http://www.monticello.org/site/jefferson/i-rise-sun.

Traill, Catherine Parr. *The Canadian Settler's Guide.* Toronto: McClelland and Stewart. 1969.

"Tulip," in Notebook [unpublished artifact] Charlotte Mason Digital Collection. Redeemer University College. http://charlottemason.redeemer.ca/PNEU- Box24/pneu162/i2p01-p37pneu162.pdf.

Van Pelt, Deani A., and Sandy Rusby Bell, "Charlotte Mason's Great Recognition." *Keynote Address*, ChildLightUSA Annual Charlotte Mason Conference, Boiling Springs, NC, June 12, 2008.

Voskamp, Anne. *One Thousand Gifts.* Grand Rapids, Michigan: Zondervan, 2010.

Waterhouse, Percy. L. *The Story of the Art of Building.* New York: McClure, Phillips & Co., 1904.

White, Gilbert. *The Journals of Gilbert White.* Edited by F. Greenoak, and R. Maybe. London: Century, 1986.

Glossary

At Table is a phrase first used by Red Mountain Community School to encompass a particular community-building practice within the school such as cooking a meal and sharing it together. In its wider sense, it implies being present to the **banquet** of a wide curriculum

Clockwise is the name of a Mason formation weekend originating with Red Mountain Community School, now one in a series known as *prov. en.der.* In its broader sense, "clockwise" is being used to refer to Mason's unhurried approach and "multiplying of time." **Timefulness** is also used to get at this part of Mason's atmosphere.

End-gaining is a term used by F. M. Alexander, to describe reaching the goal no matter how one got to it. I use **"so that"** similarly, i.e. doing something "so that" one gets a specific result.

Feast all of the relationships and idea-rich curricula resident in Mason's model. Also **Banquet**.

Forms multi-age classrooms rather than grades were used by the P.N.E.U. Students moved up less by age than by ability so this is a rough translation.

Form I (ages 6-8)

Form II (ages 9-11)

Form III (ages 12-13)

Form IV (14)

Form V (15, 16)

Form VI (17, 18)

Forms of Vitality Mason's descriptor for the various venues of self-activity in her method. (*Philosophy*, 240)

Glory simply "all the goodness of God." See also note 12.

Grand Conversation is Gordon Well's term used more and more by educators to describe "authentic, lively talk about the text" particularly in the Literature classroom. Dr. J. Carroll Smith adapts it slightly to mean the classroom discussion following a Mason lesson and narration in every subject. I am using it to indicate the handling of ideas by students of all ages grown under Mason's pedagogy and the community that builds, i.e. the younger version of **the Great Conversation** of Mortimer Adler, et al.

Great Books are the books of the Western canon identified by Adler as necessary to the Great Conversation. Mason identifies, "books the world cannot do without" in a similar way but obviously predates Adler.

Great Conversation This is Mortimer Adler's 1950's term for the questions that persist and that perennially occupy thinking people. Mason does not use this term but certainly regards the concept, calling it "the intellectual commerce of ideas." (*School*, 50-51.) I also use **Perennial Questions.**

Grand Invitation By her "masterly inactivity," Mason allows the quiet persistence of the forms of vitality to invite children to notice and discuss the **Perennial Questions,** to be delvers into existential matters for themselves. The *teleos* or end of education, as she puts it, is to become "students of Divinity."

Keeper is a person awakened to the numinous quality of notebooks.

Large Room is the end/objective of Mason's sacramental education, a full human life rich in the Knowledge of God, Knowledge of the Universe, and Knowledge of Man. The reference is from *School Education,* (171) and originally from Scripture, "thou hast set my feet in a large room" (ps.31:8).

Law of Mind Mason constructs her method on Natural Law and contends that there are things that are always true about learners that we should learn to work with and not against.

Means of Grace broadly defined as all the ways God has of imparting Grace, not just the Church's sacraments. Common Grace might be a better term, similar to Mason's use of **Glory** for all the goodness of God.

Narration is the kingpin of Mason's method. She noticed that "telling" is natural to children, and she based her whole approach on the students' re-creation of the original mind, material, or real life experience they encounter, beginning with oral language and proceeding to written work. Narration, this "act of knowing," could also encompass acting, drawing, dancing, song, etc. as the children encounter the information, thinking for themselves, and reproduce the material with their own personality stamped upon it. Thus are the children supported, "built up from within," and self-learners as the knowledge becomes their own, in the same way food is assimilated and becomes part of one's bodily life.

Nuancefulness coined word of Calvin Seerveld's; like G. M. Hopkin's "inscape," which begins to get at what Mason meant by "knowing glory."— the awareness that there is a stratum of truth beyond fact. Beauty.

P.N.E.U. Parents' National Education Union.

Perennial Questions are the questions that occupy thinking people in every generation. What is evil? How do we know? What happens after death? What is Truth? These philosophical or worldview questions and their answers down through time compose what Adler et al called the **Great Conversation.** Mason hopes to have the students in constant contact with these questions through their reading and narrating.

Person I am assuming Mason's view of the person is consistent with that of the Anglican orthodoxy of her day as created in the image of God. See also note 276.

Placefulness an awareness of the formative power of the local environment, human and natural, and stability. Wendell Berry's idea of the importance of "knowing where (we are), and the pleasures and pains of being there."

P.U.S. Parents Union School

Scaffolding is a term used by Russian psychologist Lev Vygotsky to describe the way adults may help children stand on the solid ground of what they know while they venture to build for themselves the next level of learning. At times, I am using the word more loosely, i.e. a scaffold that is not so much something that goes away after the edifice is built, though it can do that, but something that allows the edifice *to be* built, in this case, allowing a better view of **Glory**

Something True as in, "education true to the way things are," a reference to Mason's insistence on a natural law operative in education and the spiritual aspect of education.

Standing in the way of the gift is author Marilynne Robinson's term that I use to group the several expectant postures, often initiated by the notebooks, which put us in the way of an encounter with the Divine. We could also use, "doorway into the **Large Room.**"

Timefulness in Stanley Hauerwas and Jean Vanier, *Living Gently in a Violent World: The Prophetic Witness of Weakness,* the sense of having all the time one needs, unhurried, the cadence of Glory.

Notes

Preface

1   Wendell Berry, *Jayber Crow* (New York: Counterpoint Press, 2000), 160.

2   I am assuming some familiarity with Mason's basic tenets, since a full apologetic is not possible here and others have written about her ably. A newcomer to Mason may want to get a quick overview by reading Susan Schaeffer Macaulay's *For the Children's Sake*, Jenny King's *Charlotte Mason Reviewed*, or Marian Ney's *Charlotte Mason: Pioneer of Sane Education* but serious examination of Mason's educational contributions will be made through studying her six volumes on pedagogy.

3   Government of Ontario, "Grand Conversations in Primary Classrooms," *Capacity Building Series*, Secretariat Special Edition no.18 (April, 2011):1, http://www.edu.gov.on.ca/eng/literacynumeracy/inspire/research/cbs_grand_conversations.pdf. **Grand Conversation** is Gordon Well's term used more and more by educators to describe "authentic, lively talk about the text" particularly in the Literature classroom. Dr. J. Carroll Smith adapts it to mean the classroom discussion following a Mason lesson and narration in every subject. I am using it to indicate the handling of ideas by children grown under Mason's pedagogy and the community that builds, i.e. the younger version of **the Great Conversation** of Mortimer Adler, et al. (hereafter emboldened words appear in the glossary on page 158.

4   Charlotte Maria Shaw Mason, *A Philosophy of Education* (1925; reprint, Wheaton, IL: Tyndale,1989), *240*.

5   Joan Didion "On Keeping a Notebook," in *Slouching Toward Bethlehem*, (London: Andre, Deutsch, 1966), 4. I am not the first author on the subject of notebooks who has been set to thinking by Didion. Jennifer New in her

compilation of illustrated notebooks, *Drawing from Life: The Journal as Art*, (New York: Princeton, Architectural Press, 2005), 9. calls Didion's essay, "pitch perfect." I think this speaks to the point that notebook keepers often find themselves in an act of metacognition, i.e. asking, "why am I called to this practice so mysteriously?"

6   I belong in the more than one camp. I have admitted publicly to having several, no, many, personal notebooks and began what Didion calls, "this compulsion," as she suspected, when a child. I have a recipe notebook, a gardening scrapbook, a commonplace, prayer journal, nature notebook, a book of birthdays, a gratitude journal, a book list and reading journal, to name a few. What is more, reading the works of Charlotte Mason in whom I've found a kindred (paper) spirit has encouraged me in this habit. I have recently (2011) started a blog about keeping notebooks based on Mason's impetus and yes, I am aware of the irony of this.

7   Mason, *Philosophy*, 31.

8   **Narration** is the kingpin of Mason's method. She noticed that "telling" is natural to children and she based her whole approach on the students' re-creation of the original mind, material or real life experience they encounter, beginning with oral language and proceeding to written work. Narration, this "act of knowing," could also encompass acting, drawing, dancing, song etc. as the children encounter the information, thinking for themselves and reproduce the material with their own personality stamped upon it. Thus are the children supported, "built up from within" and self-learners as the knowledge becomes their own, in the same way food is assimilated and becomes part of one's bodily life.

9   Charlotte Maria Shaw Mason, *School Education* (1904; reprint, Wheaton, IL: Tyndale, 1989), 16.

10   Charlotte Mason, *Scale How Meditations*, ed. Benjamin Bernier (LuLu: 2011), 49. It would be a whole other work to explore fully what Mason means by **"glory."** There are several very good clues in the essay that contains this quote, *"Dominus Illuminatio Mea-3,"* (47-57) and I direct the reader there. For our purposes the phrase, "all the goodness of God (49) which she felt was embodied in the person of Christ, may begin to get at the sacramental notion being expressed. "'Without Him was not anything made that hath been made.' 'Hath

been' takes in all time. No true picture, poem, invention or discovery 'hath been' made for the use of man but by the "Word."' (41) **Common grace** may be another helpful term (68) or **Mystery** (83). Mason always sets the word in single quotation marks with a lower case g. I have chosen to capitalize it and leave off the quotation marks throughout to alert the reader to its numinous import.

1 – The Art of the Keeper

11   Blog authors, Bret and Kate Mackay (2010) go so far as to call the trend "the cult of Moleskine" and to distain the "faux history" associated with the company even though they celebrate the drive to keep a notebook. Bret Mackay and Kate Mackay, "The Manly Tradition of the Notebook," *The Art of Manliness*. http://artofmanliness.com/2010/08/23/the-manly-tradition-of-the-pocket-notebook/.

12   Percy Leslie Waterhouse, *The Story of the Art of Building* (New York: McClure, Phillips & Co., 1904), 9.

13   "Bookbinding" *Wikipedia*, http://en.wikipedia.org/wiki/Bookbinding (accessed Aug. 23, 2012).

14   "The Manly Tradition."

15   Waterhouse, *The Story*, 10-11.

16   Marilynne Robinson's treatment of the role of ancient literature and preliterate peoples in her essay, "Freedom of Thought," is helpful in understanding the intersection of religion, meaning-making and narrative. Robinson, *When I Was a Child I Read Books* (New York: Farrar, Straus and Giroux), 3-18.

17   Obviously this is not an academic, nor even a full treatment of the subject. I only want to notice the relationship of technology's unfolding to the human need to remember and reflect.

18   Mason, *Philosophy*, 156.

19   Ibid., 292.

20   Ibid.

21   Mason's common preface of "20 Principles" expands on these. Mason's volumes expand even further. *Home Education* collects some of Mason's earliest lectures.

22   Mason, *Philosophy*, xxvii.

23   Mason, *Home*, 240.

24   Ibid., 164.

25   "Linus Pauling," *Wikipedia*, http://en.wikipedia.org/wiki/Linus_Pauling (accessed Sept. 11, 2012).

26   R. Scott, "Galileo's Notebooks May Reveal Secrets of a New Planet," *Uninews.* The University of Melbourne. http://archive.uninews.unimelb.edu.au/view-43922.html.

27   Rutgers University, "Thomas Edison and His Papers" http://edison.rutgers.edu/papers.htm.

28   Jennifer New, *Drawing from Life,* 16. notes that Japanese women were keeping "pillow books," notebooks similar to a commonplace, which sometimes included drawings of nature, as early as the end of the 10th Century.

29   Margarita Engle, *Summer Birds: The Butterflies of Maria Merian* (New York: Henry Holt & Company, 2010).

30   Many samples of nature notebook pages made by the student teachers can be found in the Charlotte Mason Archive in Ambleside and now online through *The Charlotte Mason Digital Collection,* Redeemer University College, http://www.redeemer.ca/charlotte-mason.

31   Ilya Sandra. Perlingieri, "Paintresses: Victorian Women China Painters and Potters" *New England Antiques Journal,* March (2007), http://www.antiques-journal.com/Pages04/Monthly_pages/march07/paintresses.html.

32   "Ansel Adams," *Think Exist,* http://thinkexist.com/quotation/notebook-no_photographer_should_be_without_one/223012.html (accessed May, 2012).

33   G.E. Moulton, "The Missing Journals of Merriweather Lewis," *Journals of the Lewis and Clarke Expedition*. University of Nebraska Lincoln, http://lewisand-clarkjournals.unl.edu/read/?_xmlsrc=lc.missing.

34   J. H. Clark, "Chatelaine and Aid Memoir," *Morning Glory Jewelry*, http://www.moringglory jewelry.com/chatelaine-aid-memoire-aid-63.html.

35   University of Virginia, "I Rise with the Sun," *Thomas Jefferson Foundation*. http://www.monticello.org/site/about/thomas-jefferson-foundation.

36   Harvard University Library, "Commonplace Books," *Reading: Harvard Views of Readers, Readership and Reading History*, http://ocp.hul.harvard.edu/reading/commonplace.html.

37   Lynee Gaillet, "Commonplace Books and the Teaching of Style." *Journal of Teaching Writing*, http://journals.iupui.edu/index.php/teachingwriting/article/viewFile/1208/1169.

38   "Commonplace Books," *Wikipedia*, http://en.wikipedia.org/wiki/Commonplace_book (accessed 2011).

39   Gaillet, "Commonplace Books," 287-288.

40   Metroland News Service, "Bruce Cockburn Thanks McMaster for 'accepting all my crap.' " *Metro*, May 8, 2013, http://metronews.ca/news/hamilton/664074/bruce-cockburn-thanks-mcmaster-for-accepting-all-my-crap/.

41   Mason, *Philosophy*, 9.

42   Bernau and Buss were both closely associated with the **P.N.E.U.** (Parents' National Education Union) Bernau was a student of Mason's and Buss was Mason's peer of who founded the North London Collegiate School for Ladies. Buss likely got the history charts from Dorothea Beale. Wikipedia reports they were students together at Queen's College on Harley St. http://en.wikipedia.org/wiki/Frances_Buss (accessed May 31, 2013).

43   I am thinking here of the aftermath of No Child Left Behind in the U.S. though other western nations will recognize the debate and the mania toward testing. Mason herself did not wish to be associated with any particular educational name or movement and neither would I feel qualified to place her any particular camp.

44   New, *Drawing From Life*, 15.

45   Sharon Ely Pearson, "The New World of Curriculum Part I," *Building Faith,* On-line Christian Ed Community, http://www.buildfaith.org/2013/06/06/the-new-world-of-curriculum-part-1/.

46   Margaret Coombs, "One Comment" {on-line forum post} from http://childlightusa.wordpress.com/2012/09/09/why-homeschool-a-la-charlotte-mason-by-mary-c-gildersleeve/ (accessed Sept. 13, 2012). Kitching was Mason's long time assistant and friend.

47   Elsie Kitching "Concerning Repeated Narration," *The Parents'Review*, 31 (1) (1928): 60. Ambleside Online, http://www.amblesideonline.org/PR/PR39p058RepeatedNarration.shtml.

48   Mason, *Philosophy*, 304; *School*, 50-51.

49   Rachel Neiwert, "Savages or Citizens? Children, Education and the British Empire 1899-1950" (PhD. diss., University of Minnesota, 2009), 5. *Proquest*, UMI Dissertation Publishing, http://www.uread.com/book/savages-or-citizens-children-education/9781244071513.

50   Catherine Stonehouse and Scottie May, *Listening to Children on the Spiritual Journey* (Grand Rapids, MI: Baker Publishing, 2010), 13.

51   Mona Brooks, *Drawing with Children* and *Praying in Color* by Sybil Macbeth represent some that do approach children's work respectfully.

52   Danny Gregory, *An Illustrated Life: Drawing Inspiration from the Private Sketchbooks of Artists, Illustrators, and Designers* (Cincinnati, OH: How Books, 2008), 14.

53   Ibid.

54   Mason, *Philosophy*, 11.

55   Richard Foster, "Made Visible and Plain: On Spiritual Writing" in, *Syllable of Water*, ed. E. Griffin (Brewster, MA: Paraclete Press, 2008), 171.

56   Ibid.

2 – Gallery of Forms

57 Mason was editing *The Parents' Review* until her death in 1923. Victoria Waters, who has done considerable work with P.N.E.U materials, is confident that not much changed in the curriculum after Mason's death but I have relied mostly on pre-1923 materials to try and assemble Mason's direct views on notebooks.

58 Cholmondley, *The Story*, 71.

59 Miss O'Ferrell, "The Work and Aims of the Parents' Union School," *The Parents' Review*, 33 (11) (1922): par. 16, Ambleside Online, http://www.amblesideon-line.org/PR/PR33p777WorkAimsofPUS.shtml.

60 Lord Baden Powell, "Be Prepared," *The Listener* (1937): par. 11, The Pine Tree Web, http://www.pinetreeweb.com/bp-listener.htm.

61 Charlotte Mason, *Ourselves* Bk. II, (reprint; 1904, Wheaton IL: Tyndale, 1989), 98.

62 Mason, *Home*, 54. The words notebook and diary seem to be used interchangeably.

63 **Scaffolding** is a term used by Russian psychologist Lev Vygotsky to describe the way adults may help children stand on the solid ground of what they know while they venture to build for themselves the next level of learning. At times I am using the word more loosely, i.e. a scaffold is not so much something that goes away after the edifice is built, though it can do that, but something that allows the edifice to be built, in this case, allowing a better view of Glory.

64 Mason, *Philosophy*, 223.

65 Gilbert White, *The Journals of Gilbert White*, ed.s F. Greenoak and R. Maybe (London: Century Publishers, 1986).

66 So far there are no known **P.U.S.** (Parents Union School) student nature journals available for inspection. One can imagine that if Grandma had kept one as a schoolgirl, a family would be loath to part with it.

67 Mason, *School*, 238.

68 Ibid., 236.

69   Cholmondley, *The Story*, 273. We find this passage in Mason's *School Education* (reprint; 1904, Wheaton, IL: Tyndale, 1989), 236.

70   Used here to connote universal.

71   Cholmondley, *The Story*, 71.

72   "Tulip," in Nature Notebook, *Charlotte Mason Digital Collection.* Redeemer University College, http://charlottemason.redeemer.ca/PNEU-Box24/pneu162/i2p01-p37pneul62.pdf.

73   Again, this is a student teacher's book. Presumably they passed the habit on to their students but I have yet to find a Parent's Union School child's sample.

74   Deck, "Flower Lists" in Nature Notebook" (1910-1911) *Charlotte Mason Digital Collection.* Redeemer University College, http://charlottemason.redeemer.ca/2nd-CM-Briefcase/ALMBox127cmc519/ilp083-p158cmc519.pdf.

75   B. Rees, "Student-driven Sense-making Notebooks," *What's the Big Idea.* 9 (5): 1, The K-12 Alliance, http://k12alliance.org/newsletters/WTBI-1005.pdf.

76   Jennifer Spencer, personal e-mail to author, 2009.

77   Mason, *Home*, 265-266.

78   "P.N.E.U., School Programme 1892," *Ambleside Online.* http://www.ambleside-online.org/Programme011.shtml.

79   The importance of collecting in the before school years is elegantly described in some of the Reggio-Emilia materials. See specifically, Ann Lewin-Benham, *Infants and Toddlers at Work: Using Reggio-Inspired Materials to Support Brain Development* (New York: Teachers College Press, 2010).

80   M. Reppman, "A Few Words About the P.N.E.U." *The Parents' Review*, Vol. 12 (1901): par.13, Ambleside Online, http://www.amblesideonline.org/PR/PR12p701PNEU.shtml.

81   Ibid., "Observation and Acquaintance with Nature" section, par. 2-10.

82   The current Mason community is just beginning to configure itself in such exciting ways. Jennifer Larnder Gagnon, a veteran Mason teacher in western

Ontario, inspires educators and parents to adopt Mason's poetic approach to science through her blog, http://belikefabre.blogspot.com/.

83   Mason, *Home*, 86.

84   Jennifer Spencer, personal e-mail to author, 2009.

85   "P.N.E.U Specimen Programme of a Term's Work, 1921," *Ambleside Online*. http://www.amblesideonline.org/FormI.shtml.

86   Mason, *Philosophy*, 218.

87   K. Hugman, "House of Education Natural History Notebook *1922*," *Charlotte Mason Digital Collection*, Redeemer University College, http://charlottemason. redeemer.ca/Box22/cmc147/il-p92cmc147.pdf. It is not clear that Mason has any hard and fast rules here but it would seem important that students continue keeping a Nature Notebook, if modern science teaching and University entrance demands separate lab books for modern seniors.

88   Mason, *Home*, 54.

89   Red Mountain Community School has designed and sells a beautiful Book of Firsts. See information under Resources. Either a Calendar or a Book of Firsts or a combination of these means, seem to address the need Mason presents as long as it is understood that "Firsts" means in the natural world. This is not the place to record the first lost tooth or first bike ride or even the first battle on American soil. Other notebooks do that.

90   "The Gods of the Copybook Headings," *Wikipedia*, http://en.wikipedia.org/ wiki/The_Gods_of_the_Copybook_Headings (accessed June, 21, 2012).

91   Mason, *Home*, 235.

92   Ibid., 238.

93   Ibid. This is not a book for students' creative writing as we understand it and which Mason little encouraged. Mason's students did eventually write poetry but more as a noticing of a certain style or type of poetry or as a narration at exams on certain topics. Mason sees that "creative writing assignments" are disrespectful; children need to read and copy from the greats first and the creativity would arise naturally from that exposure and her unique use of narration. Mason, *Home*, 243.

94   By yearbook we understand a daily diary like a current "day planner" rather than the book of class pictures and autographs known to modern high school students.

95   Mason, *School*, 135.

96   "P.N.E.U. Programme 1922," *Ambleside Online*. http://www.amblesideonline. org/Programme94VI.shtml.

97   Brush drawing was a scheduled activity but I have yet to find archival evidence of illumination to support this speculation.

98   Unfortunately I cannot recall where I read this. I don't think it was a constant practice.

99   Digital copy work would likely not have the same effect. That doesn't mean that Mason would have eschewed the computer, just that copy work has a different purpose and atmosphere and therefore requires pen and paper. In my blog, http://www.bookofcenturies.com/, I do gather quotes electronically for the purpose of showing what can go into Mason's various notebooks but I have written or drawn first in most cases.

100   Luci Shaw, "The Writer's Notebook" in *Syllable of Water*, ed. E. Griffin (Brewster, MA: Paraclete Press, 2008), 29.

101   Mason talks about this painting at length in *Ourselves* Bk II, 41-48, and fortitude seems to be something she felt was particularly missing in that generation--one wonders what she might say of this generation. If one was making a fortitude journal, the painting would make a good cover. (Likewise, making one's own notebook would be a good handicraft.)

102   Mason, *Ourselves*, Bk. II, 47.

103   Webster, 1998 ed.

104   Ann VosKamp, *One Thousand Gifts* (Grand Rapids, MI: Zondervan, 2010) has made popular a similar notebook, a Gratitude Journal, in our day.

105   Mason, *Philosophy*, 50.

106   Shaw, as cited in Griffin, 27.

107 Mason, *Ourselves*, Bk II, 47.

108 There is evidence of its use in **form IV** and up.

109 Charlotte Maria Shaw Mason, *Formation of Character* (reprint; 1905, Wheaton IL: Tyndale House Publishers Inc, 1989) 260.

110 "*PNEU Programme, 1922.*"

111 It would be lovely to see a P.N.E.U student's copybook or Commonplace but I am unaware of a sample. Chances are, like the rest of the student-generated work, these became family heirlooms that were highly treasured. This would account for the scarcity in the archive.

112 "George Washington's School Copybook," *Reason.* American Treasures of the Library of Congress. http://www.loc.gov/exhibits/treasures/trr048.html.

113 "*P.N.E.U Programme, 1922.*"

114 Mason, *Home,* 315.

115 "P.N.E.U. Exam 94," (1922), *Ambleside Online.* http://www.amblesideonline. org/Exam94IV.shtml .

116 What happened physically to written narrations is still somewhat unclear in all subject areas, and that may have to do with the "scores" of ways a narration could be undertaken. We know every lesson had its immediate narration. Elsie Kitching makes a clear distinction between a "composition" that came later (maybe even later in the week or term) and the common narration that nurtured the habit of attention in every child. (Kitching, "Concerning Repeated Narration," par.5.)

117 Mason, *Philosophy,* 337.

118 Mason, *Home,* 222.

119 Ibid., 203.

120 Mason, *Home,* 301.

121 I am thinking here of Francois Gouin's method of Language Acquisition, which Mason says she relied upon heavily. (*Home,* 302-307.) In brief, all of Mason's practice in Language Acquisition followed this natal pattern, supporting

language first in the ear, (hearing) then in the mouth (speech), next in eye (reading) and last in the hand (writing). I am grateful for discussions with Dr. Jennifer Spencer about Mason's reliance on Gouin.

122   Charlotte Maria Shaw Mason, *Parents and Children*, (reprint; 1896, Wheaton IL: Tyndale House Publishers Inc., 1989.

123   Again, year-book connotes something similar to our typical "datebook" or journal. (or perhaps today a Blackberry.)

124   Mason had a great deal to say about character formation and moral training all through her writings, and this paper does not allow for that discussion except to say in this context that the parent, who might begin with a young child using this year-book, will, ideally, gradually make over the care of his moral life to the child, allowing ever greater levels of responsibility for the inner landscape whilst steering him or her away from the "morbid act of introspection."(*Parents*, 207).

125   Mason, *Philosophy*, 131.

126   Mason says in the preface to *Ourselves* that Book I is for middle to upper school age children under 16. No doubt the intent is for a slow working through the ideas over several years and numberless conversations. Book II is for young adults 16 and above, then.

127   This idea came from a private conversation with Kristy Fittro, daughter of Susan Schaeffer Macaulay. Fittro had a cottage school education based on the work of Mason and describes the scroll the students drew, episode by episode, after hearing readings of *Pilgrim's Progress*. She still has the scroll as a keepsake.

128   Mason, *Philosophy*, 131.

129   Being struck by the passage above a few years ago, I determined to notice "The Way of the Will" more in my teaching and created an actual chart. A copy is included in the appendix. "The Way of the Will" might be noticed incidentally in discussions and readings by younger children, but *Ourselves* (Bk. II) deliberately teaches "the two secrets of moral and intellectual self management," "The Way of the Will" and the "Way of Reason," to students over age 16 after they have had many years of historical and literary examples of "choosing" following Mason's usual pattern of naming a thing after it has been experienced. To use

such a chart with younger children would, in my estimation, be counterproductive and possibly harmful. (Mason, *Ourselves*, preface.)

130   Mason, *Formation*, 259.

131   "Enquire Within Upon Everything," *Wikipedia,* http://en.wikipedia.org/wiki/ Enquire_Within_Upon_Everything (accessed 2011).

132   Catherine Parr Traill's, *The Canadian Settler's Guide*, written in 1855 may be representative of this sort of writing.

133   "Parent's National Educational Union Reading Course," *Charlotte Mason Digital Collection,* Redeemer University College, http://charlottemason. redeemer.ca/2nd-CM-Briefcase/Box48/Box48cmc371/i1p1-p5cmc371.pdf .

134   H.W. Household, "P. N. E. U. Methods of Teaching with Special Reference to the Teaching of English," (London: P.N.E.U., n.d.), 3. *Charlotte Mason Digital Archive*, Redeemer University College, http://charlottemason.redeemer. ca/2nd-CM-Briefcase/Box16/cmc107/II/ilpl-i2p3cmc107II.pdf.

135   Mason, *Home*, 240.

136   Mason, *Philosophy*, 273.

137   Mason, *Ourselves,* Bk. I, 37.

138   Mason, *Home., 292.*

139   Cartridge paper was a tough, usually unbleached paper used for endpapers, linings, and shotgun shells from whence it takes its name. The term "cartridge paper" is not generally used in the United States. What we know as "Tag stock" or Bristol board may be similar. Sheets of Cartridge paper sold today come in various sizes; one such standard is approximately 23 x 33." For our purposes, it is enough to imagine a largish piece of stiff paper.

140   Mason, *Home*, 281.

141   D.M.H. Nesbitt, "The Teaching of History," *The Parents' Review*, 12 (1901): 917-929, Ambleside Online. http://www.amblesideonline.org/PR/ PR12p917TeachingofHistory.shtml .

142   Mason, *Philosophy*, 177.

143 Dorothea Beale, "The Teaching of Chronology," *The Parents' Review* 2 (2) (1891/92) :81-90, Ambleside Online. http://www.amblesideonline.org/PR/PR02p081Chronology.shtml, para.23.

144 Ibid.

145 R.A. Pennethorne, "P.N.E.U. Principles as Illustrated by Teaching," *The Parents' Review*, 10 (1899): 549, Ambleside Online. http://www.amblesideonline.org/PR/PR10p549PNEUPrinciplesIllustrated.shtml,Par.61.

146 Mason, *Home*, 292.

147 Beale, "The Teaching of Chronology." Par.13.

148 H.B. "History: Teaching Practically Considered." *The Parents' Review*, IV, (1993/94): 890-896. Ambleside Online. http://www.amblesideonline.org/PR/PR04p890History.shtml .

149 I recognize that this is a precarious argument; more research needs to be done on Mason's use of timelines and charts and the archive will likely continue to reveal clues. For now I simply wish to make the point that there are various principles being upheld in her use of such tools and that the tools themselves might be adapted to the child's need. There are slight differences between these two authors which I am not able to explore here, but both seem to support the progress from known to unknown, building time sense gradually, using increasingly complex or symbolic time tools.

150 I am thinking here of the careful observation required in Nature Study, Picture Study and the like and the training of the eye in language through copy work and dictation.

151 H.B. "History Teaching," par.16,

152 I don't read these as strict "developmental stages."

153 And these are not a straight linear progression but an overlapping or even spiraling usage that is not demonstrated well by my graphic.

154 Mason, *Home*, 279-280.

155 Working on The Child's Own History Chart does not preclude the child from "reading" (or being read) stories and tales from times other than his own. He

continues to gather his time sense from these readings, but they are not added to this chart.

156 Thomas Armstrong, *The Best Schools* (Alexandria, VA: Association for Supervision and Curriculum Development, 2006), 132.

157 Beale, "The Teaching of Chronology," par. 14.

158 Ibid.

159 H.B., "History Teaching." One thinks of Francis Schaeffer's "flow of history."

160 Beale, "The Teaching, of Chronology," par.9.

161 Mason, *Philosophy*, 176.

162 Beale, "The Teaching of Chronology," par.9.

163 H.B., "History Teaching," par.11.

164 Winifred Irving, "Notes on Making a Time-line," (London: Parents National Educational Union, n.d.), *Charlotte Mason Digital Archive*. Redeemer University College, http://charlottemason.redeemer.ca/2nd-CM-Briefcase/Box16/cmc107/I/i3l-p4cmc1071.pdf.

165 Ibid.

166 Ibid.

167 G.M. Bernau, "The Book of Centuries." *The Parents' Review* 34 (1923):720-724. Ambleside Online. http://www.amblesideonline.org/PR/PR34p720BookofCenturies.shtm.

168 Mason, *Philosophy*, 175-6.

169 "P.N.E.U. Programme, 1922."

170 O'Farrell, "The Work."

171 I have recreated a Book of Centuries based on these descriptions. Details are given under Resources.

172 G.M. Bernau, *The Book of Centuries and How to Keep One,* (London: Parents National Education Union, n.d.), Charlotte Mason Digital Collection. Redeemer

University College. http://charlottemason.redeemer.ca/2nd-CM-Briefcase/Box17/cmc113/p001-p070cmc113.pdf

173   Ibid., 8.

174   Ibid., 1.

175   Ibid., 5.

176   Ibid., 8.

177   Ibid., 5.

178   Bernau, "The Book of Centuries," (1923).

179   Eve died in 2004.

180   G.M. Bernau, "Century Books," in *Parents' Union School's Diamond Jubilee Magazine*, (1951):42-44. Charlotte Mason Digital Archive. Redeemer University College. http://charlottemason.redeemer.ca/@nd-CMBriefcase/Box17/cmc113/p001=p070cmc113.pdf.

181   "P.N.E.U. Programme, 1922." shows this for all terms and forms III and IV but the directive is typical in those years for the programmes we have access to.

182   C. S. Lewis' Introduction to *Athanasius: On the Incarnation*, trans. Sister Penelope Lawson, The *Spurgeon* Archive, http://www.spurgeon.org/~phil/history/ath-inc.htm#ch_0.

183   Mason, *Ourselves*, Bk. II, 11

184   Mason, *Philosophy*, 124.

185   Ibid., 124.

3 – The Grand Invitation

186   Mason, *Parents and Children*, 1.

187   Matthew B. Crawford, *Shopcraft as Soulcraft: An Inquiry into the Value of Work*(New York: Penguin Press, 2009), 21.

188 **End-gaining** is a term I first encountered in F. M. Alexander, to describe reaching the goal no matter how one got to it. Alexander is founder of the "Alexander Technique," a method of education,often used by performers, that teaches students to work with (and not against) their musculature, for breathing, oration and health.

189 Mason, *Philosophy*, 240.

190 Ann, Lewin-Benham, *Infants & Todddlers*, 11.

191 I have learned to be respectful to the student who has not given his best attention with this phrase of Melanie Walker-Malone's.

192 Summerhill was a British educational thrust known for giving children democratic powers within the school.

193 Armstrong, *Best*, 48.

194 R.N. Caine, G. and others, ed.s 12 *Brain/Mind Learning Principles in Action: Developing Executive Functions of the Human Brain,* 2nd ed. (Thousand Oaks, CA: Sage Publishing, 2008), xii.

195 "Georgia O'Keefe," *Brainy Quotes,* http://www.brainyquote.com/quotes/g/georgiaok134583.html. (accessed December 23,2011).

196 At first, times for using certain of the notebooks will need to be scheduled. Eventually the teacher will say after a lesson, is there anything you would like to put in your Book of Centuries or Commonplace?" and finally the student will herself suggest, "I want to put this in my Nature Notebook" or "I need time to draw this in my Book of Centuries."

197 Paradigm shift is a modern term. Mason talks about wanting an "inverted order of things" based on a Christian perspective. Mason as cited in Bernier, *Meditation*s, 50.

198 "Paul Coelho" *Brainy Quote,* http://brainyquote.com/quotes/authors/p/paulo_coelho.htm (accessed December 23, 2011).

199 Mason, *Philosophy,* 149.

200 B. Rees, "Student-driven Sense-making Notebooks." *What's the Big Idea, 9 (5)* (2010): 1, http://k12alliance.org/newsletters/WTBI-1005.pdf.

201   Gaillet, "Commonplace Books", 287.

202   Andrew Gudgel, "Commonplace Books—Old Wine in New Bottles," *Andrew Gudgel's Writing Blog*, http://andrewgudgel.com/commonplace.htm.

203   Gaillet, "Commonplace Books," 287.

204   Mason, *School*, 271.

205   M. Koker, D. Duquin and K. Burke, "Frequently Asked Questions about Science Notebooks," *Center for Educational Innovation Public Education Association*, http://sites.google.come/site.ceipeascience/research-on-science-notebooking.

206   Crawford, *Shopclass*, 15.

207   Armstrong, *Best*, 101. An interesting proposal of why this might be the prevailing atmosphere in our classrooms is Neil Postman's account of how the West came to hold technology as a deity in his 1992 work *Technopoly*.

208   Armstrong, *Best*, 102.

209   "Marshall McLuhan." *Wikipedia*, http://en.wikipedia.org/wiki/Marshall_McLuhan (accessed October 22, 2012).

4 – "Setting Up Self-activity"

210   *Postman, Technopoly, 147.*

211   *Mason, School, 65*

212   Mason was known to say that the good teacher looks like he is doing very little.

213   Mason, *Home*, 160.

214   Mason, *Philosophy*, 217.

215   Rebekah Brown Hierholzer, personal e-mail, 2009.

216   Mason, *School*, 239.

217 I mean copy work to imply all the ways things are exactly reproduced in a Mason education, from transcribing the alphabet correctly and beautifully to reproducing a line of music, a map, an algebra problem or even learning to reproduce part of a great painting, all those things may end up in notebooks and are practices in a Mason school, but the main method and content of the notebooks is narration. Copy work is closely related but practices attention with the eye and hand, and not so much the memory.

218 It seems living a typical Mason school day is one of the fastest ways of bringing parents to student work with knowing eyes. In practicing the methods themselves, parents and teachers begin to know how much personal effort is involved and what satisfaction is gained, even when there is relatively little "evidence" of the lesson.

219 Lewin-Benham, *Infants and Toddlers*, 13.

220 Cholmondley, *Story*, 70

221 Mason, *Home*, 313.

222 Cholmondley, *Story*, 71. Many of the few notebook resources available for children I reviewed seem to suggest that the preprinted pages must be structured, even busy, with drawings, instructions and enticements, to interest children. While not exactly what Mason would call "twaddle," such tactics are not necessary to the process Mason seeks and may even subvert attention and relationship. At best, teachers might use these types of books themselves to get ideas for fieldwork or "special studies," keeping in mind Mason's rule of thumb, "all important things are simple."

223 Mason, *School*, 80.

224 Mason, *Home*, 54.

225 Mason, *Home* 86; *Formation*, 341.

226 Mason, *Philosophy*, 340. Again, Neil Postman, *Amusing Ourselves to Death*, (New York: Penguin 1984) is an invaluable perspective on this discussion.

227 Wendi Capehart, "Learning Styles and Graphic Media," *Ambleside Online*, http://amblesideonline.org/BooksPicturesshtml.

228 Mason, *Home*, 21.

229 Nicholas Carr, "Is Google Making us Stupid? *The Atlantic*, August, (2008) http://www.theatlantic.com/doc/200807/google.

230 Mason, *School,* 230.

231 Wendell Berry, *The Art of the Commonplace: The Agrarian Essays of Wendell Berry,* ed. N. Wirzba, (Washington, Shoemaker & Hoard, 2002), 74.

232 Quentin, J. Schultze, *Habits of the High-Tech Heart: Living Virtuously in the Information Age,* (Grand Rapids, MI, 2002), 18.

233 Hopefully more research will clarify how often notebooks were used and how much freedom to add to these books the children had.

234 Before they come to **Form I**, Mason hopes children will have as much experience with things *in situ* (*School,* 214) as possible and a wide experience with materials. (Mason, *Home,* 315.) Again, Lewin-Behham makes a compelling case based on Vygotsky's theories.

235 Bernau, "The Book of Centuries," (1923).

236 Bernau, *The Book of Centuries and How to Keep One*, 8.

237 Bernau, "The Book of Centuries," (1923).

238 Gudgel, "Commonplace Books."

239 These recommendations have been borne out through my own teaching experience but also rely on discussions with and the unpublished work of Rebekah Brown Hierholzer, Deborah Dobbins, and Holly Anne Dobbins.

240 Bernau, *The Book of Centuries and How to Keep One.*

241 untitled article, Karen Andreola, ed. *The Parents' Review*, 1, (winter): 1.

242 Mason, *Home,* 130.

243 Didion *Slouching,* 140.

244 Rees, "Student-driven," par.1.

245 Mason, *School,* 183ff.

5 – "R.S.V.P. The Shape of Life

246   Hannah Hinchman, *A Trail through the Leaves: Journal as a Path to Place,* (IL: W. W. Norton & Company, 1999) 8.

247   Ibid., 10.

248   Mason, *Home,* 69, 265.

249   Mason, *Formation,* 305; Kieran Egan, *Children's Minds, Talking Rabbits & Clockwork Oranges,* (New York: Teachers College Press) 92; Reinhold Niebur as cited in James Houston, *Joyful Exiles: Life on the Dangerous Edge of Things,* (Downers Grove, IL: Intervarsity Press, 2006) 66.

250   Thomas Armstrong argues in *The Best Schools* against educationfor "high test scores" and for "personal fulfillment" (154). While Armstrong's call for a wider more human education is very welcome, his view appears to be more individualistic than what Mason posits.

251   Mason, *Ourselves,* Bk. II, 70, 172.

252   Mason, *Parents,* 242.

253   New, *Drawing,* 9.

254   Gaillet, "Commonplace Books,"

255   Cholmondley, *Story,* iii.

256   Mason, *Ourselves* Bk. II, 178.

257   Mason, *School,* 90.

258   Mason, *School,* 171.

259   James K. A. Smith, *Desiring the Kingdom: Worship, Worldview and Cultural Formation,* (Grand Rapids: Baker Academic), 18.

260   Mason, *Philosophy,* 266.

261   Schulze, *Habits,* 35.

262   Armstrong, *Best,* 135.

263   Cholmondley, *Story,* iv.

264   Mark Hederman, *The Boy in the Bubble: Education as Personal Relationship* (Dublin: Veritas, 2012).

265   Richard Foster, *Celebration of Discipline*, 25th Anniversary. Ed. (San Francisco: Harper, 1998), 7. Foster is using **"means of grace"** broadly and more sacramentally than just the sacraments of the Church. See glossary.

266   Benjamin Bernier in Charlotte Mason, *Scale How Meditations,* Benjamin Bernier, ed. (LuLu), 128.

267   Mason, *Parents,* 271.

268   Benjamin Bernier, posting to Charlotte Mason Series discussion list, "CM Series, 03 Notes on the Heart," January 4, 2013, http://groups.yahoo.com/group/CMSeries/message/14364.

269   Bernier in Mason, *Meditations*, 11-12.

270   The whole of this unique chapter should be read. i.e. Mason, *Parents*, 268-279.

271   Mason, Parents, 271. Nancy Pearcy treats this idea of the divided self based on Francis Schaeffer's work in *Saving Leonardo* (2010) with an obvious Christian perspective, as do Ranald Macaulay and Jerram Barrs in *Being Human* (Downer's Grove, IL: IVP Academic, 2005) but "personhood theory" is a rich discussion of our times in many sectors and will resurface continually as one studies Mason. I am assuming here Mason's view of the **person** is consistent with that of the Anglican orthodoxy of her day as Bernier has argued.

272   Mason, *Ourselves*, Principle 18, Introduction. It may be hard for us to conceive Mason 's conception of "divine Spirit" here: she notes that many other cultures were aware of the mystery of education and the divine nature of knowledge. Her epistemology is rooted in, but does not seem to require, a Christian definition. (Mason, *Meditations*, 44,51,56) As C.S. Lewis' does in *Mere Christianity*, (London: Fontana,1963), 39., Mason's Great Recognition allows for the workings of the Divine in the lives of *all* persons, no matter what faith. Mason has a Christian notion of God, but her generosity and humility seem to allow a lot of room for a person's concept of God to differ from her own as evidenced by the rich relationships within the P.N.E.U. Henrietta Franklin, for instance, was a devout liberal Jewess.

273 Ibid., *Ourselves,* Bk. II, 177.

274 Charlotte Maria Shaw Mason, "The Reading Habit and a Wide Curriculum," talk prepared for unknown presentation, 23, *Charlotte Mason Digital Collection,* Redeemer University College, http://charlottemason.redeemer.ca/PNEU-Briefcase/PNEU-Box04/pneu49/i04p01-p25pneu49.pdf.

275 Mason, *Parents*, 104.

276 "Lectio Divina," *Wikipedia*, http://en.wikipedia.org/wiki/Lectio_Divinia (accessed Jan. 13, 2013).

277 Foster, *Celebration*, 72-73.

278 Mason, *Philosophy*, "A Short Synopsis," xxxi.

279 Mason, "The Reading Habit," 19.

280 Mason, *Ourselves*, Bk. II, 174.

281 Mary Ann Schaffer and Annie Barrows, *The Guernsey Literary and Potato Peel Pie Society*, New York: Dial Press, 2009. This is not to suggest "desultory reading" which Mason was against. (Mason, "Reading," 7.)

282 "Lectio Divina."

283 Postman, *Technopoly*, 111-122; Schultze, *Habits*, 7.

284 Mason, as cited in Bernier, *Meditations*, 36.

285 Mason, *Home*, 265.

286 This is not to say that the oral narration does not do these things too. Indeed, most times the oral narration precedes the notebook work and often makes it unnecessary. The child is not being asked to narrate the same thing twice.

287 Robinson, *When I Was a Child*, 3-18.

288. Calvin G. Seerveld, Rainbows *for the Fallen World*, (Toronto: Tuppence Press, 2005), 145.

289 Ney, *Charlotte Mason*, 29

290   Mason, *Philosophy*, 18-19. Of course adding a nature notebook habit would be valuable in and of itself. One must start somewhere and presumably each step toward a more vital practice is a step in the right direction.

291   Obviously, students receiving an education based on Mason's design have been few in this century and consequently studied very little since her re-emergence. My own anecdotal experience with students "brought up" under Mason's methods are very convincing and I am anxious to see Mason's method revived as fully and completely as possible and look forward to the results of such endeavors with great expectation and hope.

292   Armstrong, *Best*, 71.

293   Metzger, "More Lyrics" *Doggie Head Tilt*, http://www.doggieheadtilt.com/more-lyrics/#more-1141.

294   Obviously this balance of left and right brain support is found through-out her method and not just with the notebooks. It is clear that while providing for variety in lessons and plenty of acknowledgement of the students' bodily-ness, Mason is not recommending children needing to have *only* motor education early in order to prepare them for intellectual work. (Mason, "Reading,"14.

295   Vigen Guroian, "Awakening the Moral Imagination: Teaching Virtues through Fairy Tales." *The Intercollegiate Review* (Fall 1996).

296   Mason, *Home*, 152 ; Vigen Guroian,"*Tending the Heart of Virtue*," (London: Oxford University Press, 1998); Sir Ken Robinson, "Imagination and Empathy," *Educating the Heart*, The Delailama Center, http://www.youtube.com/watch?v=Yu2zcmb3yAQ

297   I am using "Other," in the sense that Martin Buber uses it, to signify the human importance of relationship and not in the derogatory sense of them/us. Martin Buber, *I and Thou*, Walter Kaufman, trans. (New York, Charles Scribner & Sons: 1970).

298   Mason, *Philosophy*, 133.

299   Mason, *Ourselves*, principle 17. I realize Mason's idea of an ethically based education, a practice defined by what is right and not by what is expedient, is rare in this culture where everything is considered valuable for its ability to "work" or produce a result. A case in point is Dr. Kelly McGonigal's very

popular Standford course "The Science of Willpower" and the ensuing book, *The Willpower Instinct.* (New York: Avery, 2012). McGonigal explores the neuroscience behind "willing," adding much to back up Mason's treatment in *Ourselves,* but testifies to the flavor of this generation's "so that" posture, i.e. "I study and understand willpower *so that,* I can (fill in the blank) "succeed in my law degree, lose weight, stop smoking etc. etc." rather than, "I employ my will because it makes me more fully human to choose rather than to react." This **"so that"** attitude seems to me precisely where we go wrong in education and what Mason is fighting against. We would think it an abuse if we fed a child the best food available "so that " she could be shaped into the next Miss America; we feed her because she is hungry and the nourishment is life-giving. So, too, knowledge, whether about chemistry or what comprises a human person we offer because the child is hungry for it; it is her birthright. This is not to say that the data McGonigal assembles will not be of use in helping people overcome difficult situations or in our further understanding of the human mind and heart, just that the propensity for disrespecting a person is always subtly present with the power of knowledge.

300   Mason, *Meditations,* 118.

301   Mason, *Home,* 152.

302   **"Clockwise"** is the name of a Mason formation retreat originating with Red Mountain Community School, now one in a series known as prov.en.der. In its broader sense, "clockwise" is being used to refer to Mason's unhurried approach and "multiplying of time."

303   Schultze, *Habits,* 18.

304   Obviously this is a "First World" problem. It may be that cultures with less ability to purchase technology are discretely blessed by their lack in this instance.

305   Thomas Armstrong, *Best,* 128., notes the critical need for such "expressive" practices and the use of "heirloom" books by Clarkson School of Discovery, a middle school in North Carolina.

306   Education may devolve into "A List" that emphasizes having "had" all the Great Books in an almost promiscuous sense of conquering rather than being changed by a book. Mason's pedagogy is "**clock wise**" precisely because transformation takes that much time and we must always be "fitted to a book." (Mason, *Formation,* 382; *School,* 340.)

307   Berry, *The Art,* 81.

308   Schultze, *Habits*, 68.

309   Sarah Bestvater personal correspondence with the author. 2013.

310   Armstrong, *Best*, 73, 82.

311   Frank Partnoy, *Wait: The Art and Science of Delay*, (New York: Public Affairs Press, 2012), xi.

312   Victor, Frankl, *Man's Search for Meaning*, (New York: Pocket Books, 1963), 191; Francis Schaeffer, *True Spirituality*, 30th Anniversary ed. (Wheaton, Ill, Tyndale House Publishing, 2001), 12.

313   Partnoy, *Wait*, xi.

314   Mason, *Ourselves*, Bk. II, 165.

315   Partnoy, *Wait*, xii.

316   Ibid., 14.

317   Mason, *Meditations*, 194.

318   Mason, "The Reading Habit," 20.

319   Partnoy, *Wait*, 227.

320   Ibid., 214.

321   Ibid., 215.

322   The Church knows this as Kairos time--a Greek work meaning, "a time when conditions are right for the accomplishment of a crucial action: the opportune and decisive moment." (Merriam Webster, on-line ed., "Kairos.")

323   Ibid., *Wait,* 230.

324   I first came across this word, **timefulness,** in Stanley Hauerwas and Jean Vanier, *Living Gently in a Violent World: The Prophetic Witness of Weakness,* (Downer's Grove, IL: InterVarsity Press Books, 2008). I do not know who coined it, but like **nuancefulness** it is very apt in discussing Mason.

325   Partnoy, *Wait*, 245.

326   as cited in New, *Drawing*, 65.

327   Hinchman, *A Life*, 98.

328   Ibid., 95.

329   Gary Brown, as cited in New, *Drawing*, 104.

330   Mason, *Philosophy*, 224.

331   Carol, Beckwith, as cited in New, *Drawing*, 99.

332   K. Margolis and S. Trimble, "Paying Attention: An Interview with Barry Lopez." *Orion*, http://arts.envirolink.org/interviews_and_conversatons/Barry Lopez.html; Berry, as cited in Wirzba, *The Art*, 2002.: Mason, *Philosophy*, 224.

333   Berry, as cited in Wirzba, *The Art*, 96.

334   Mason, *Philosophy*, 224.

335   Mason*, Parents*, 188. A picture book that introduces **placefulness**, noticing, and where things come from is *Agatha's Featherbed* by Carmen Agra Deedy, illustrated by Laura L. Seely. It teaches a delightful refrain, considering where things come from. This is a nice example of how the forms of vitality can be flexible: An "Everything Comes from Something" notebook or at least a page in the Nature Notebook, or Enquire Within, could be begun for **Form** I listing things like silk comes from worms, cotton comes from bols, wool comes from sheep, to be added to as discoveries are made.

336   Mason, *Home*, 67.

337   Phyllis Lassner and Lucy Le-Guilcher, *Rumer Godden International and Intermodern Story Teller.* (Burlington VT: Ashgate Publishing, 2010), 191.

338   Rumer Godden *China Court: The Hours of a Country House,* (New York: William Morrow and Company, 1960/61), 37-38.

339   Mason, *Parents*, 188.

340   Mason, *Home*, 72.

341   Berry, *The Art*, 5.

342   I first heard this question posed by Melanie Walker-Malone head of Red Mountain Community School. RMCS has done a superb job of recognizing the importance of place and the particularities of Alabama in the life of their school.

343   Mason, *Ourselves,* preface, 42.

344   Mason, *Meditations.* 66.

345   Mason, *Philosophy*, 253- 257.

346   Mason, *Philosophy*, 224.

347   Ibid., 278.

348   Mason, *Meditations,* 95.

349   Schultze, *Habits*, 53.

350   Mason, *Meditations*, 69.

351   Mason, *Philosophy*, 277.

352   Mason, as cited in Bernier, *Meditations*, 48

353   Victor Frankl as cited in E. E. Smith, "There's More to Life than Being Happy," The Atlantic, Jan. 9, 2013, http://www.theatlantic.com/health/archive/2013/01/theres-more-to-life-than-being-happy/266805/.

354   Dr. Kelly McGonigal *, The Willpower Instinct*, 24.

355   Barbara L. Fredrickson, "Your Phone vs. Your Heart," *Sunday Review,* New York Times, March 23, 2013, http://www.nytimes.com/2013/03/24/opinion/sunday/your-phone-vs-your-heart.html?_r=0.

356   While this term, "fencing the table," can be used to suggest a church's "closed communion," a practice of restricting the Eucharist to only members of a certain congregation or denomination, I am using it here in its broadest, most allegorical sense. In other words, a "good fence" would protect the essence of the encounter and the inherent hospitality and gracefulness of the **Feast**, but not restrict people from participating.

357   Hauerwas and Vanier, *Living*, 69.

358   Ibid., 48-49.

359   Ibid., 104.

360   Schultze, Habits, 48, 57; Vanier and Hauerwas, *Living*, 17.

361   Mason, "The Reading Habit," 4.

362   Armstrong, *Best*, 73, 82.

363   Ibid., 71, 80, 128.

364   J. Carroll Smith, "Introducing Charlotte Mason's Use of Narration," *Forum on Public Policy*, summer (2008): 2, http://forumonpublicpolicy.com/summer-08papers/archivesummer08/smith.carroll.pdf.

365   Armstrong, *Best*, 39, 41.

366   Ibid., 78.

367   Ibid., 46, 131, 140.

368   Ibid., 103,125,136.

369   Mason, "The Reading Habit,"19.

370   Armstrong, *Best*, 125, 130.

371   Ibid.,103, 112, 120.

372   Ibid.,104.

373   Armstrong, *Best*, 117, 132.

374   Ibid., 60.

375   Mason, "The Reading Habit," 8.

376   Esther de Waal, *Seeking Life: The Baptismal Invitation of the Rule of St. Benedict* (Collegeville, MN: Liturgical Press, 2009), 32.

377   "The Legend of the Leprechaun," *Irish Blessings*, http://www.irishindeed.com/page.htm?pg=LEPRECHAUN%20MYTH.

378 Mason, *Formation*, 313.

379 Mason, "The Reading Habit," 23.

380 De Waal, *Seeking Life*, 36.

381 Schulze, *Habits*, 61.

382 Mason, *Meditations*, 19.

383 De Waal, *Seeking Life*, 40.

384 Mason, "The Reading Habit," 22.

385 **At Table** is a phrase first used by Red Mountain Community School to encompass a particular community-building practice within the school such as cooking a meal and sharing it together. In its wider sense, it implies being present to the banquet with all the relationships that implies.

386 Mason, *School*, 182.

387 as cited in New, *Drawing*, 70.

388 Mason, *Meditations*, 83.

389 Marilynne Robinson, "Marilynne Robinson: Prevenient Courage," *Faith and Leadership*, Duke Divinity School, http://www.faithandleadership.com/multi-media/marilynne-robinson-prevenient-courage.

390 Berry, *The Art*, 2002, 297; Foster, *Celebration*; Hauerwas and Vanier, *Living Gently*; Schultze, *Habits*.

391 Mason, *Meditations*, 51.

392 Esther De Waal, *Seeking God: The Way of St. Benedict* (Collegeville, MN: Liturgical Press 2001).

393 Berry, *The Art*, 23.

394 Kentz as cited in New. *Drawing*, 72.

395 "The Glory of God is Man Fully Alive," *Ten Thousand Places*, http://tenthou-sandplaces.org/2009/04/25/the-glory-of-god-is-man-fully-alive/.

396   Mason, *Ourselves* Bk. II, 177; Mason, as cited in Bernier, *Meditations,* 73.

397   Hinchman, *A Life in Hand,* 15.

398   Mason, *Meditations,* 56.

399   Ney, *Charlotte Mason,* 48.

400   Cholmondley, *The Story,* 34.

401   Hauerwas and Vanier, *Living Gently,* 104.

402   Mason, *Meditations,* 42.

403   Hauerwas and Vanier, *Living Gently,* 56.

404   Mason as cited in Bernier, *Meditations,* 22.

405   Ibid., 148.

"We are here to abet creation and to witness it, to notice each thing, so each thing gets noticed...so that creation need not play to an empty house."

– Annie Dillard

Made in the USA
Coppell, TX
20 September 2023

21802808R00118